2.00

To Norma -
My "Greatest" Partner

John -
Christmas
1965 -

The Walk of the Oysters:

AN UNHOLY HISTORY OF CONTRACT BRIDGE

by Rex Mackey

Prentice-Hall Inc., Englewood Cliffs, N. J.

for Carmel

ACKNOWLEDGMENT

The stanza on page 112 is taken from 'Who Taught Caddies to Count' by Ogden Nash, first published in the New Yorker, © *1947 by Ogden Nash, quoted by permission of the author.*

First published in Great Britain
by W. H. Allen, London, 1964

First American Edition 1965
Second printing .... December, 1965

Library of Congress Catalog Card Number: 65-10134

Printed in United States of America

T   94434

Prentice-Hall International, Inc., *London*
Prentice-Hall of Australia, Pty., Ltd., *Sydney*
Prentice-Hall of Canada, Ltd., *Toronto*
Prentice-Hall of India (Private) Ltd., *New Delhi*
Prentice-Hall of Japan, Inc., *Tokyo*

Foreword

It seems ironic to me that the only rejection slip I have received in modern times had to do with a piece I composed on an Alice in Wonderland story. The rejection came from a periodical which I hold in the highest esteem, and rather than have my efforts go for naught, I submitted the product to an English publication who accepted it with alacrity.

When Mr. Mackey asked me to do the foreword to his *The Walk of the Oysters,* I was inclined to give him a friendly warning, but decided against it. So, here I am again, attempting to be a collaborator of Lewis Carroll. It is gratifying to be able to return the kindness that was shown me in Dublin several years ago, when with Helen Sobel and two Yorkshire men, I made up a team to compete against the Irish Internationals in Dublin. While it was our good fortune to win this contest, it was only after stubborn resistance from the home team, which at times threatened to subdue us completely. The occasion stands out in my mind, because of a compliment which the author paid me in Dublin. I had suggested to one of my hosts that I should like to pay a visit to the Blarney Stone, and Mr. Mackey suggested in a moderate sort of way that that would amount to carrying coals to Newcastle. Our match with the Irish Internationals was quite memorable, and I had hoped that we might be invited to return to the Emerald Isle for a re-play of the contest. So far, no invitation has been forthcoming, and it appears that I shall have to be satisfied with this contribution, though I shall complain vigorously to my team captain, Ewart Kempson, the distinguished editor of *Bridge Magazine.*

I ask you to join with me in appreciating the color of Mr. Mackey's offering which I hold in the highest esteem.

CHARLES H. GOREN

Contents

"O Oysters, come and walk with us!"
  The Walrus did beseech.
"A pleasant walk, a pleasant talk,
  Along the briny beach:
We cannot do with more than four,
  To give a hand to each."

Tweedle-Dee in *Through the Looking Glass*

by **LEWIS CARROLL**

1

Vanderbilt Deals

The natural instinct of the social historian, in Europe at any rate, is to treat the year 1925 with silent contempt. It was the time of the great hangover. Despite the affable gentlemen who signed the Locarno Treaties "forever preserving their nations from the scourge of war," everywhere there was unemployment, crises, confusion, and gloom, gloom, gloom. If it is true that time does not exist for the sick, the year was a chronological hyphen. Perhaps in fairness it should be recorded that in Germany a rising young author had prescribed the panacea in a textbook called *Mein Kampf,* and in Italy the trains had begun to run on time.

Far otherwise, however, was the scene in the United States. The President was Calvin Coolidge, the same whose death was later to occasion Arthur Mizner to inquire, "How do they know?" Like an indulgent father who does not wish to be disturbed, he surveyed his merry-making children with a benign if impassive eye. And so, to the sensuous strains of the ukulele the family of Uncle Sam sang *Bye-Bye Blackbird* and went on a glorious binge. While the Rum Fleet lay offshore, New York became a vast speakeasy; the civic affairs of Chicago were guided by the competent hands of Alphonso Capone; in the deep South the Dayton Monkey Trial put the Bible in the ring against the *Origin of Species;* and on a November night

1

in his stateroom on the *S.S. Finland,* Harold Sterling Vanderbilt shuffled a pack of cards.

In itself this was hardly a notably dramatic action, and least of all on the part of Vanderbilt for whom this form of exercise was anything but a novelty. Nor did his remark when riffling the cards seem to be in any way momentous; yet it is entitled to a place in any anthology of famous first words because it marked the birth of a legend.

He said, "Gentlemen, let me show you a new game. It may interest you."

Now, it should be said at once that the genesis of Contract Bridge is lost in the mists of a controversy which has not been resolved by the experts contradicting not only each other, but themselves.

For instance, Charles H. Goren, the present king of bridge, says in the 1960 edition of the *Encyclopaedia Britannica* that "Contract Bridge was introduced into the U.S.A. by way of France around 1927." In the next breath, as it were, he announces in the 1961 edition of *Collins Encyclopaedia* that "During a steamship voyage from Los Angeles to Havana in November 1925 a small group of players fixed the basic features of the game. Vanderbilt has been conceded to be more responsible for the creation of the game than anyone else."

In the last edition of *Hoyle,* Ely Culbertson also attributes the invention of the game to Vanderbilt, but in 1926; but what are we to make of the circumstantial article in the 1962 edition of *Encyclopaedia Britannica* over the names of Culbertson and his associate, Alfred H. Morehead?—"Contract Bridge was not a new game when in the 1920's it suddenly became popular. It was played in the United States as early as 1915 and the committee on the laws of the Whist Club considered incorporation of the contract bridge principle into the auction bridge laws in the version of 1917 and again 1920. They refrained because they thought such a difficult game would forfeit the popularity of auction bridge."

"In 1926 Harold S. Vanderbilt of New York, on a cruise in

2

the Caribbean, played Plafond games on shipboard. A young lady, whose name he later forgot, suggested that a side winning a game be vulnerable. In the course of the trip Vanderbilt devised the modern scoring table, with its large slam bonuses with the factor of vulnerability included. By 1927 this scoring schedule had made contract bridge popular; by 1928 contract bridge had all but supplanted auction bridge among the leading American players, and was widely played in the British clubs; by 1929 it had become the standard game on both sides of the Atlantic."

Compare this with the *International Celebrity,* U.S. Edition of 1961 which informs us, "In 1926 on board the *S.S. Finland,* bound from San Pedro, California to the Canal Zone he invented the game of Contract Bridge. 'The scoring and other features of the game which I invented at that time,' he says, 'and which were used by myself and three other friends are almost identical with those used today. The word vulnerable was originally suggested by a young lady passenger on board, whose name I cannot remember, but she had played some other game in which the term was used.' After inventing the game Vanderbilt had to overcome the indifference of a public which was playing auction bridge (if it was playing at all). Soon, however, he did so; he added extra points for slams, increased penalties for going down etc."

In the 1946 edition of *Hoyle* the immortal R. F. Foster dismisses the matter with hardly a backward glance, "a form of Contract Bridge first made its appearance in 1921 . . . but it was short-lived."

Finally, in 1933, Lieutenant - Colonel Walter Buller, the despot and creator of British Bridge, proclaimed that he and he alone was the onlie begetter of the game.

Well, it is all very mystifying! Apparently the ancient legal maxim that there are liars, damn liars, and expert witnesses, is not without foundation. Two things, however, emerge clearly; firstly, that the game in its present form can be definitely attributed to Vanderbilt, and secondly, that he devised it aboard ship. When this evidence is related to the verified fact that the *S.S. Finland* was not in the Caribbean in 1926, but was on a Hawaiian cruise in November 1925 a common denominator, as it were, of the versions of the anonymous contributor to the U.S. *Celebrity Register,* Goren's in 1961, and Morehead's in 1962, coupled with Vanderbilt's own comments appear to give us the true facts of the case. The discrepancy of a year in the Register may be accounted for by the fact that while the cruise started late in 1925 it did not finish until early 1926. Further, in his *Contract Bridge,* the first textbook ever written on the game, published in 1929 and now quite invaluable, Vanderbilt's dedications reads:

> To My Friends, Frederic S. Allen, Francis M. Bacon 3rd., Dudley L. Pickman Jnr., to Whose Co-operation is Due the Evolution of Contract Bridge Scoring.

From this tribute we may reasonably infer that we have discovered the names of the good companions who were in the stateroom when the seal was broken on the fateful pack.

Lives of all great men remind us that practically every great discovery is an unpremeditated fluke. It is understandable therefore that when asked considerably later, Vanderbilt could recall only the general circumstances of the accouchement of Contract Bridge which have hitherto been so uncertain, for he was a man of many parts and many interests. Scion of the fabulous clan whose wealth is rooted in American history, Harold Sterling, otherwise "Mike" Vanderbilt, needed no pedigree to establish a title to fame in his own right. In the period between being a wartime naval commander (destroyers) and a railroad king, three times he successfully defended the Americas Cup, in 1930 with *Enterprise* against Tommy Lipton and in '34 and '37 against that other famous Tommy—Sopwith—with *Rainbow* and *Ranger.*

"Mike" Vanderbilt was just as much at home with the *avant*

4

garde on the Left Bank, as were his parents with Edward the Seventh and the Kaiser. When his sister, Consuelo, by her spectacular marriage converted Blenheim Palace into a frozen asset of the New York Central Railroad he had himself inadvertently become brother-in-law to the Duke of Marlborough.

This was the man then whose diffident remark to his shipboard cronies became historic. For the new game did interest them—very much.

It also interested untold millions whose numbers are still expanding. Housewives, who had hitherto thought a dummy was a baby's pacifier, banded themselves together to the permanent ruin of their husbands' digestions. It interested newspapers and publishers, films and radio, big business and ballyhoo merchants. It added a new dimension to leisure, and it also provoked murder, mayhem and domestic strife; the marriage of its greatest exploiter finished in the divorce courts where it had long before established a new hymeneal discord.

Whatever may be in dispute, of one thing we may be certain, on that tropical night in the Pacific Vanderbilt had cleared the deck for Contract Bridge.

From at least the middle of the seventeenth century Whist, and later its derivatives, was played in England. Originally a strictly upper-class pastime, during Dickensian times it penetrated the green baize doors and became, and still is, the game of the so-called working classes.

Then in 1894, in the most famous of all card clubs, the Portland, the game of Bridge was introduced by Lord Brougham, who had played it in India with some Indian Army officers. It differed radically from the parent game in that the Dealer or, on his refusal, his partner, named the trump. Stake points could be doubled or redoubled *ad infinitum,* no trumps could be announced, and most radical of all, the Declarer's partner's hand was exposed after the first lead. This was known as the Dummy hand.

A code of Rules and Etiquette was drawn up by the Portland

Club which, like the Jockey Club, became in more ways than one the Lords Justice of Appeal.

Despite this introduction, the genesis of this, the earliest form of the game, is even more obscure than that of Contract, the very derivation of the word "Bridge" being doubtful. Hitherto no authority has ever collected available evidence on the subject; perhaps the omission can be remedied.

As to the origin of the name, there is a pamphlet in the Bodleian Library at Oxford, the only copy in existence, in which the term occurs for the first time. This was anonymously published in 1886, and is entitled "Biritch or Bridge Whist, or Russian Whist," and describes the main features of the game which it says is a variation of the Russian game of Vint. The Russian attribution would be more plausible if there were a word Biritch in that language, but there is not. Possibly it was a Slavonic mode of address to a female partner.

The *Harmsworth Encyclopaedia* for 1906 tantalizingly informs us that it was played in Constantinople in 1860, and blandly leaves it at that, coyly refraining from disclosing its source, or any other authority for these remarkable data. It is as well to remember that Harmsworth was also the publisher of such authoritative periodicals as *Answers* and *Tit-Bits*.

The *New Universal Encyclopaedia* is just as infuriating: "the first recorded game seems to have been in Constantinople in 1874. Its earliest appearance in the United Kingdom was probably among the Greek colony in Manchester around 1880."

And again the blanket of silence descends.

There is, however, one piece of evidence which is at least first hand and circumstantial. Writing to the *Bridge Magazine* in May, 1932, Frank J. Nathan describes himself as the survivor of the first Four to play Bridge in England, and identifies the other three as his father, Jack Sefton Mayers, and a Colonel Studdy. The last named, he tells us, when he introduced the game to the Nathans and Mayers, said it was of Levantine origin, and that he had learned it in the trenches at Plevna during the Russo-Turkish War of 1877-78.

The four of them played it at the St. George's Club, Hanover Square, London, and in the winter of 1892 the Club set aside a special table for Bridge. This has all the stamp of verisimilitude and would appear to explode the accepted theory that its initiation to the Portland Club was the first appearance of Bridge in English card rooms.

Whatever the truth, and whatever its provenance, whether Russian, Turkish, Greek or Indian, as from 1894, when Lord Brougham brought it to his fellow members' attention, the popularity of Bridge was immediate, the combination of skill and speculation proving irresistible to the players of the older game. After ten years or so, however, these very qualities proved the seeds of its doom, and Royal Auction Bridge in turn superseded it.

The essentially different feature of Auction lay in the right of every player at the table to bid until the other three players had passed. The last bid suit then became trumps, and the innovation "no trumps" was, of course, retained. Furthermore, only the partnership which had won the auction could score points towards the game, their opponents could only score penalties for defeating them. As in Bridge, there were bonus points for honor card holdings, making small and grand slams, and (most important) the Rubber bonus which went to the side first making two games.

While Auction became a widespread vogue, the avalanche was yet to come. Miss Nancy Mitford does not mention its having been played in the Hons' cupboard, but it might have been, without loss of caste—it was very, very U, as indeed was its predecessor. Furthermore, the protagonists of the game considered that the *ne plus ultra* in card games had been reached. They were wrong, for while the reign of Auction lasted a few years longer than the Thousand Year Reich, any extant specimens of Auction Bridge players are probably catalogued in the Natural History Museum in South Kensington. They had not reckoned on Harold S. Vanderbilt's South Sea voyage and coming events had not yet cast the ominous shadow of Mr. Ely Culbertson.

For the die-hard Auction players, however, as far back as 1919 a tiny cloud, no larger than the deuce of clubs, had already appeared on the horizon. The French, who have invented as many cards games as they have forms of government, had thought up a form of Bridge which they christened Plafond. This was and is an excellent, but difficult, game which combined the best features of Auction with the refinement that only such number of tricks as the final bidder had announced he would obtain could count towards the game, and so towards the Rubber bonus. Auction demanded no such accuracy. If the bidding died at, say, One Spade and the Declarer proceeded to make Four, he scored his game just as if he had bid them; this was naive and pleasant for sweet old ladies and retired warriors at the nineteenth hole, who found it difficult to add up to four anyway. According, the apologetic attempts to introduce Plafond into England were met with the same sturdy resistance as their grandfathers had accorded the Reform Bill.

It was the historic pattern: invasion from the Continent failed, but the real menace threatened from the seceded colonies in the West. As with all good Americans, the ubiquitous Mr. Vanderbilt's spiritual home was in Paris, and at the Traveller's Club there he had tasted the joys of Plafond. Hence that memorable Rubber beneath the Southern Cross.

He called his new game Contract Bridge. He drew up a code of rules, which with minor variations apply today. He evolved a system of scoring, which has been altered from time to time in scale, but not in principle. Above all, he succeeded in obtaining the imprimatur of the Knickerbocker Whist Club of New York, the Portland Club of America.

He was then propelled, not off the stage, nor rudely—one is not rude to a Vanderbilt—but decisively and firmly in the direction of the wings by an unknown young Russo-Scots-American named Culbertson.

8

2

Ely Opens the Bidding

Ely Culbertson was what his contemporary, Damon Runyon, could and did describe as a character. He was a product of the era, and what an era! Enough has been written about the America of the bull market, the hip flask, the cement waistcoats, and defenestrating financiers falling like ticker tape on Wall Street to make comment superfluous. Culbertson, an exotic plant, came to full bloom in a propitious climate.

In 1925, Ely Culbertson was thirty-four years of age: he was also nobody in particular. The child of a Russian mother and a Scots-American father who had helped to found the Grozny Oil Field on the Caspian Sea, he had been educated by tutors and in various European universities. Having married Josephine Murphy Dillon in 1922 in New York he continued to live there in that twilight of frugal luxury which is an Eleusinian mystery to economists, toilers and tax collectors.

For his future activities the theatrical metaphor is happiest. When the curtain rose on Contract Bridge, Culbertson, hearing the cue for his grand entry, bounded nimbly and unerringly right to the center of the stage. Before anyone really realized what was happening he had appropriated the limelight, the footlights and the orchestra as well. When he became impresario he did not disdain to act as stage manager, and indeed he was shortly to become an adroit scene-shifter.

Extracurricularly, he taught himself Contract Bridge.

Now, Culbertson was not by a long chalk in the front rank of New York card players. As a Poker player (although, typically, he wrote a book on it) Arnold Rothstein would have told him to go and play Old Maid. Even in his selected field of Bridge, to mention only a few names at random, the great R. F. Foster, Sidney Lenz, P. Hal Sims, or Vanderbilt himself, were much better players, and for that matter, much better writers. But Ely had something that was worth a great deal more than the concentrated skill and felicity of all his rivals put together. As a showman and psychologist he was well up in the Barnum class, and when he felt the national temperature he found it was feverish, not to say febrile.

The great American public would buy literally anything, and fall for anything. Large tracts of Florida, most of it sand, and a great deal of it under the Atlantic Ocean, were sold for millions; as a desirable slice of real property Brooklyn Bridge found ready purchasers.

It was the same with fresh sensations. Any form of new aberration, innocuous or otherwise, was assured of success—and that meant financial success. There had been Mah Jongg, an unbelievably tedious game with Chinese Dragons, Poetic Winds and mumbo-jumbo generally which infected the country like a plague; another appalling game called Monopoly in which were bought large holdings in shipping lines, oilwells, textiles and the like appealed to those who also played the Stock Market, which was the entire population over the age of puberty. Culbertson rightly felt that people who would play Mah Jongg would play anything. He made them play Contract Bridge. If comparatively few of them have ever succeeded in playing it particularly well, largely thanks to him, they have nevertheless played it in their millions ever since.

Culbertson's impact, dynamic as it was, was merely a prelude. Together with the pyrotechnics to come it formed part of a ruthless and widespread invasion of private life. His influence was incalculable, and when he was later described as

the Emperor of Bridge he had earned his title by right of con-
quest and expropriation. For years, and for innumerable
players, the terms Bridge and Culbertson were so interchangeable that it is only in the context of his activities in the field
he made his own that such a transformation of social habits
can be explained.

Ely and Jo, as they became known to their devotees, discovered Contract in 1927 in New York. Jo was already an
Auction teacher and her husband supplied the jam on the daily
bread by judicious play in the clubs. Immediately realizing the
potentialities of the new game, he set about spreading his
theories. He wrote free articles for magazines and house and
hotel organs. He gave lectures. The new broadcasting stations
were at their wits' end for material, Ely supplied it for nothing.
He played with old ladies for a cent a hundred, and with tough
crap and poker guys of Broadway, but this was only prepara-
tion. The impact came in October 1929.

In the previous summer through a friendly lawyer who
waited for his fee, and as a result made a fortune, Culbertson
turned himself into a corporation and acquired dingy premises
at 45 West 45th Street, leased to him by an understanding
landlord. With the background of these imposing assets and by
a combination of fast talk and hard neck he bemused printers,
publishers and distributors into coming across with a three-
month credit. Then came the most fantastic stroke of luck of
all. Quite unknown to Culbertson, his only possible competitor, the *Auction Bridge Magazine,* was broke. The September
issue was its last; it went bankrupt and put up the shutters.

In October the first issue of Ely's brainchild *The Bridge
World* dedicated to Contract and the proprietor's crusade, had
the field to itself, and it did not neglect the majestic situation
which to this day it occupies. Its success was immediate. The
first issue sold 3,000 copies, the entire printing. The staff (of
two) were paid, the landlord and publishers were handed
checks and bootleg decoctions in a downtown speakeasy by
the new President, Board of Directors, Editor and contributors,

11

all of which diverse functions were discharged by the versatile proprietor. The sordid cares of credit and rent were forgotten. The impact was made!

Next on the schedule was the real invasion. At that time Culbertson was almost unknown. The acknowledged authorities in the States were such figures as the revered doyen, R. F. Foster, Milton Work, who invented a point count of evaluation still in world-wide use, Sidney Lenz, who had recently published the best book on Auction ever written, and was the world's best player, and a number of other top-class writers with their systems and admirers. These formed the Establishment, and it had money, tradition and respect. Culbertson, the Outsider, had none of these, but he had a flair and showmanship and, through his *Bridge World,* a unique and powerful advantage.

At almost the same time as Culbertson's advent, a rather more sinister bandmaster in Germany achieved the world's headlines, and, while fortunately their objects differed, the identity of their methods is amazing. With a disarming effrontery, Culbertson has told us how he planned for, and succeeded in, making himself and his system omnipotent.

At the outset he required Group Leaders; his own expression. These were people drawn from Society, sporting circles and the like, who could spread the gospel by word of mouth, a medium in which Ely was both adept and enthusiastic. Then came a body, actuated by mixed motives, made up of their own self-interest and belief in his theory. From them he recruited his authorized teachers, three thousand of them, each armed with a Culbertson Teacher Diploma in black and white and gold, issued under the sign manual of the master. Finally, came an amorphous collection which had one common denominator, undiluted greed. This included authors, lecturers, club owners, newspaper and radio executives, department stores and business organizations. In time Culbertson had them all working for him, and, need it be added, very much for themselves as well.

His approach to capturing the mass mind, again his expres-

12

sion, sounds more like assault although he called it appeal. This fell under three main headings: Ego, Fear, and Sex. His reasons for working on these three basic foundations are illuminating.

Ego. The green baize table is the great leveller. The office boy and the tycoon have equal rights in the pasteboard republic, indeed the office boy can be boss. Furthermore, American womanhood achieved its rightful place as man's superior. With more time on her fair hands, which also held the moneybags, she got the full propaganda blast and generally became a better player than her husband. Jo, the housewife's pinup girl, became a symbol.

Fear meant sanctions against the non-player. He was persuaded that Bridge was a social necessity. If he played well he was invited everywhere and met the right people, and the contrary applied. Only one System could teach him. He learned it at the feet of the lawgiver.

Sex. Quite deliberately he invented Bridge terms with an eye to opening the door to naughty jokes, puns and shocked feminine giggles. His own System was the Approach Forcing. Soon the country was talking about Squeezes, Take-outs, Vulnerability, One over One, Going to bed with my Jack and so on. The husband and wife, sweetheart and lover angle was fully exploited; it was left to other and profane pens to record the blazing rows between himself and Jo, and the acid wisecracks of his swift-tongued Irish spouse.

It was decided to take stock at the end of the first quarter of 1930; *The Bridge World* was then exactly six healthy months old. The balance sheet might not look so healthy to an accountant, but its proprietor was satisfied. From the very first he had decided that unto him who hath publicity all things shall be added: and so he was satisfied. His great plan was working beautifully; each month thousands of letters were answered and hundreds of teachers, having passed their examination, were awarded the accolade of a diploma; the Group Leaders played Culbertson in New York, Miami and Hollywood, while the teachers taught.

Big business had yet to surrender, but in the meantime the three Fates of Ego, Fear and Sex were spinning their web about the victims. Each month in *The Bridge World* had been announced the forthcoming publication of the *Blue Book*. This authority, it was modestly claimed, would be the definitive masterpiece through which alone the truth would be revealed. If the date of publication was withheld there were two good reasons which the author did not think fit to disclose. In the first place, it was his deliberate policy to inflame the public into a state of unbearable anticipation, in the second place, not one word of it had been written.

What Culbertson, ever the gambler, was really waiting for was a break. Intuitively, he realized that he needed just one shattering explosion of publicity in which to discharge his book, and his fortune was made. Even he, the arch-priest of the improbable, never for one moment foresaw the quarter from which the bonanza was to beckon.

In that very month of March, 1930, in faraway England Lieutenant-Colonel Walter Buller, retired, Companion of the British Empire, sometime officer on the staff of Field Marshal the Earl Haig, recking not its import, gave utterance to the following pronouncement: "American methods are unethical in principle and worthless in practice. I feel that a good British four could be got together to take on the Americans and that, while not necessarily the best available, they would beat them sky-high."

This was more than good enough for Mr. C. It is difficult to read a firm challenge into Buller's soldierly bombast, but Culbertson treated it as an affront to Old Glory comparable to the burning all over again of the White House by the licentious redcoats. The April issue of *The Bridge World* sizzled on the printing presses. The Colonel's alleged challenge was proudly accepted. The Editor himself and three others would take on the might of Empire anywhere at any time, and the sooner the better. He asked for no terms; they would pay all their own expenses; to eliminate luck they would play three hundred duplicate hands for no stakes, or for any stake, and they would play the Culbertson System.

This modest reply to the transatlantic defiance was sent also to all the English and American dailies and the delighted newspapers gave it front page treatment. Millions of readers who had never played Bridge in their lives became patriotic partisans ovenight. Poor Buller had no choice. He could either play up or shut up. He played up.

The preliminary sparring was strictly for the publicity boys; the issue could not now be evaded, and the date of conflict was fixed for the week beginning Monday, September 15, 1930; the venue, the historic Almacks Club in London. None knew better than Culbertson what was at stake; it was no less than his entire future.

Just what had he taken on?

In 1919 a half-baked form of Plafond came over from France with the returning officers, but it fizzled out. In May 1926 A. E. Manning-Foster founded the *Auction Bridge Magazine,* and in 1929 he printed the word "Contract" on its cover, but he placed it second. The roster of contributors to this organ, which reads like a lengthy extract from the Army List, indicates the class to which it catered. The early volumes feature articles by no less than one General, eight Colonels, five Majors and four Captains. The silent service, appropriately, was represented by merely one Captain and one Lieutenant-Commander R.N.

The diffident recognition of Contract in the magazine was an acknowledgment of the infiltration of the new game, and that people were eager to know more about it. Also in obedience to the demand, Manning-Foster himself wrote a very bad book on it, as did Buller, who advocated a fatuity of his own invention called "British Bridge," which he claimed was founded on common sense and natural methods. As correspondent for the *Star* and other publications, the Colonel—who was no mean publicist himself—induced a number of patriotic disciples, both writers and players, to take it up. By 1930, as a result, "British Bridge" was making a fair amount of money, especially for those who did not play it.

It is hard to believe that David Low had not met Buller before he created Colonel Blimp, although one is almost persuaded that Colonel Buller was a caricature of Blimp rather than vice-versa. He was indeed perfect of his kind, if a little larger than life, as a few of his utterances will show:

On himself:
"I am the most successful bidder in the world."
"I am totally lacking in vanity."

On Culbertson System:
"Its followers are bumblepuppies, quacks. The Cumbersome System consists of artificial stunts which must be eschewed, the product of sub-human system-mongers. The sooner we cut out this nonsense the better. Even the village idiot would accept this, but not the bridge world."

On Culbertson:
"There is no hope for the future of the game until we can do something to alter the parochial outlook of those (like him) who seek to control it."

"Culbertson is not strictly a Bridge player, his fans should take up Rummy."

On British Bridge:
"American Bridge is made up of farcical stunts and fantastic codes which can be compared with the two-eyed stance and bad play of the young cricketer. Players of British Bridge condemn these practices as childish, unscientific, and often unethical."

and again:

"No one can accuse me of bigoted nationalism. I like a man for what he is (and sometimes a woman). I do not care

a fig whether he is a Russian, an American, or even an Irishman (I am half-Irish!). I want the best in Bridge, and I do
not find the best in America. Advocate British Bridge. Thanks
to me it is not too late."

His philosophy was summed up by his henchman, Major J.
Buckley, D.S.O., M.C.:

"I am absolutely convinced that the British people are the
greatest natural players in the world. They have a flair for
the game and a card intelligence possessed by no other race
of people. Mechanical systems, although admittedly helpful
to the American mentality, have created a state of chaos in
British Bridge. Restore British Bridge the prestige and
power which is its rightful inheritance."

This sort of thing of course brought sweetness and light to
cynical editorial hearts on both sides of the Atlantic, and the
headlines reacted accordingly. It is a matter of statistical fact
that the forthcoming match rated more column coverage than
any previous sporting event, not excepting the famous Tunney-
Dempsey return fight in 1927. A coverage only to be surpassed
by Culbertson himself in his later exploits.

In the interim Ely had to think and move fast. Jo was terrified out of her wits. Despite the progress of the master plan,
and the publicity, there were days when they literally had not
a dollar. And they needed at least $5,000 for England, exclud-
ing fares. As to that, Culbertson had already, through *The
Bridge World,* put over a deal with the French Shipping Line,
as a publicity stunt ostensibly for their mutual benefit, but
which in fact resulted in himself and his fellow players obtaining free stateroom travel on the *Normandie* as guests of their
unwilling, but committed, hosts.

For months Ely had been plugging the *Blue Book,* the im-
pending answer to a Bridge Player's prayer. Now he announced
its publication date, September 15 which, by an amazing coincidence, corresponded with the opening day of the Great Match

in London. As a special concession, open only to faithful
readers of *The Bridge World* who filled in the attached form,
he offered autographed copies at $1.50, instead of $2 unauto-
graphed after publication. They subscribed nearly $10,000
almost by return of post, leaving Mr. Culbertson exactly six
weeks in which to write and publish his magnum opus.

Jo was aghast. "Now," she said, "if you don't write it you go
to jail."

Fear of incarceration was not the only spur. With a typical
brashness, having discovered the cupidity of publishers, he had
already formed his own publishing company, which meant
that, after expenses, every cent of the sales of the *Blue Book*
went into his own pocket.

With the help of the unflagging Jo, a distracted army of
secretaries, typists and printers, no sleep, and gallons of black
coffee, somehow the copy was set up. There was not even time
to correct the galley proofs properly. The last fortnight was
spent dictating from a hospital bed. He dictated the final page
in a taxicab on the way to the dock, and even shouted the
dedication, "To my wife, my favorite partner," from the ship's
rail.

As the *Normandie* moved slowly down the Hudson, Ely and
his team went to the bar. Jo had a double. There was little
Culbertson could now do except hope that the match would
stay on the front page in England.

He need not have worried. His ebullient opponent saw to
that end of it. In 1930 England was becalmed in one of her
perennial sporting doldrums. Larwood and Jardine had not yet
invented body-line bowling and imperilled the Empire. Bobby
Jones had just completed his immortal Grand Slam. It would
be three long years before Perry and Austin were to win the
Davis Cup. Phil Scott had made the horizontal championship
his very own. All was gloom, deep and unrelieved. At no time
since the Great War had the country so badly needed an international boost at any game whatsoever.

To the news editors of Fleet Street Buller was a godsend, and his "British Bridge" became the weapon with which to repel the all-conquering Yanks' and vindicate national honor. The scribes and photographers descended on Southampton like locusts.

We may date the meteoric rise of Contract Bridge as an international phenomenon from the moment the American team stepped ashore. The fact that neither team had the right to represent its country mattered not at all; the news agencies, the newspapers, and the newsreels, saw to it that the public was committed to a patriotic orgy. And that is the way it was; and stayed.

When the reporters fired their questions at Culbertson his replies were, for him, unassuming and deprecatory, although they did not come out that way in the wash. When he read the interviews the following morning it was to find them bespattered with "Gee Whiz," "Gosh," "Youse got sumpin' baby," and so on. This maddened the cosmopolitan Ely who thought he had behaved at Southampton with an urbanity worthy of Lord Chesterfield. When he held pre-match court in his suite at the Carlton he decided to give the Limey press what it obviously wanted.

"What is your opinion of the British team's chances, Mr. Culbertson?"

"About the same as a snowball in Hades."

"Oh! It has no chance?"

"Not a chance. It doesn't play the Culbertson System."

"What do you think of British Bridge?"

"Look fella, let's keep the party clean."

"How about Colonel Buller as a player?"

"You heard my last answer!"

"Who, in your opinion, is the greatest living player?"

"Me."

"Are there any other great players?"

"Yeah! The rest of my team."

This maddened Buller, but the pressmen went off squealing like happy schoolgirls.

The choice of venue for the great event was an inappropriate stroke of genius. In the spacious days of the Regency, Almacks was the center of rank and beauty where congregated "The Rulers of Fashion, The Arbiters of Taste, The Leaders of *Ton,* and the Makers of Manners." It is unfortunate that there were no interviews with the astonished ghosts of Fox and Sheridan, Brummell and Lady Jersey, even Prinny himself.

The American team consisted of Culbertson and Jo, Theodore A. (Teddy) Lightner and Baron Waldemar von Zedwitz, a German aristocrat now an American citizen. They were faced by Lieutenant-Colonel Buller, Mrs. Gordon Evers, Doctor Nelson Wood-Hill, and Cedric Kehoe. Both sides appreciated the value of the feminine element, not but that either lady could hold her own in the sternest male company. The ladies of the press and their readers were also duly appreciative, as were the playing card manufacturers.

About the actual match itself there was a strange dichotomy. On the one hand there was the surprising decorum of the players who outdid each other in politeness, although roped off from the spectators like boxers in a ring; on the other, was the note of near hysteria on which the proceedings were reported on each side of the Atlantic. While this was exultant in London after the first day when Britain led by a few hundred points, it reached its crescendo after the second.

Afterwards, that day was described sepulchrally by Buller as The Black Tuesday of British Bridge. In the two sessions' play the Americans had turned their deficit into an unbelievable lead of over seven thousand points. This proved decisive, for nothing the British did could make a significant inroad on such an impressive balance.

Tom Webster produced a caricature depicting a disconsolate lion in Buller's likeness. A shower of playing cards are falling from his nerveless paws, and the caption reads *Cricket, tennis, golf and now this!* Harsh, but true.

If it was Black Tuesday for Buller, it was in a very different sense the turning point of Culbertson's life. From New York he received a cable:

BLUE BOOK OUT STOP FIRST EDITION SOLD OUT TWENTY
FOUR HOURS STOP SECOND THIRD EDITIONS NOW PRINTING
ALSO SOLD OUT SUCCESS ENORMOUS STOP YOU ARE RICH

Even now he could not relax. Defeat could kill the sales of
the *Blue Book* stone dead; as he said himself later it could have
been the end just at the start of the beginning. After the avalanche of September 16, however, only unimaginable disaster
could bring defeat; disaster did not strike and he cruised to a
comfortable victory of 4,845 points. (In those medieval days
the no-trump counted 35 points.) He then accepted a friendly
challenge from another warrior, Lieutenant-Colonel (Pops)
Beasley, with a team composed of members of the famous
Crockford's Club, and beat him by 4,905.

This was merely a social relaxation, there was nothing much
at stake except a welcome boost to the already blazing publicity. In addition, he was glad to use the extra time the match
afforded him to fertilize the virgin English market. Buller admitted six years later that when Culbertson sailed back to the
States in 1930 he had not only achieved international publicity,
he had converted and recruited hundreds of thousands of
players to his system and to his book. Duplicate Bridge was
introduced, to be played to the present day in ever increasing
numbers. True to his principles, he formed his *corps élite* of
Group Leaders, and laid the foundation of a nationwide organization of teachers.

In this last regard, he told a rather pathetic little anecdote.
When packing for his return, a diffident little man was shown
into his suite. It was Doctor Lasker, the all-time great chess
master, whose name is part of the history of the game. He
asked haltingly for a teacher's diploma, he said he could pass an
examination. Culbertson was dumbfounded.

"Please, Mr. Culbertson, it is very important to me to have
a diploma. I am not very rich."

With a not very characteristic humility Culbertson gave him
one. There was no examination.

BULLER v CULBERTSON
Almacks, London, 1930

SOUTH DEALS.

BOTH VULNERABLE.

```
                      NORTH
                      ♠ Q J 7 5 4
                      ♥ 7
                      ♦ J 6 5
                      ♣ 10 8 6 4
         WEST                          EAST
         ♠ 9                           ♠ 8 6 2
         ♥ A K 6                       ♥ 10 5 4 3
         ♦ K Q 10 2                    ♦ A 8 4
         ♣ A J 9 7 3                   ♣ K Q 5
                      SOUTH
                      ♠ A K 10 3
                      ♥ Q J 9 8 2
                      ♦ 9 7 3
                      ♣ 2
```

Room 1

South	West	North	East
Von Zedwitz	Buller	Jo	Mrs.
1 ♠	Double	Culbertson	Evers
		2 ♠	All pass

Result: 8 tricks made

Room 2

South	West	North	East
Kehoe	Culbertson	Wood-Hill	Lightner
1 ♠	2 ♥ (!)	No(!)	3 ♥
No	4 ♥ (!)	No	No
Double	No	4 ♠ (!)	Double
All pass			

Result: Down 2

This bidding is not invented. Whatever about the bidding, or lack of it, in Room 1, that in Room 2 shows the experts in their full refulgent bloom. Four hearts doubled can be beaten three tricks, but presumably out of courtesy to his distinguished guests, Wood-Hill "corrects" to Four Spades which goes down two. This represents a swing of 1300 points.

It may be pointed out that Game in Diamonds or Clubs cannot be defeated, neither of which suit receives even a passing mention in either room.

BULLER v CULBERTSON
Almacks, London, 1930

DEALER SOUTH.

LOVE ALL.

NORTH

Mrs. Culbertson

♠ 9 6 4 2

♥ 3

♦ A K Q 7 3

♣ 10 4 2

WEST

Col. Buller

♠ A J 10 7

♥ J 10 9 6 5

♦ J 9 5 2

♣ —

EAST

Mrs. Evers

♠ K 5

♥ K Q 8 2

♦ 10 4

♣ A J 9 8 6

SOUTH

Von Zedwitz

♠ Q 8 3

♥ A 7 4

♦ 8 6

♣ K Q 7 5 3

South	West	North	East
1 ♣	—	1 ♦	—
—	Double	—	1 ♥
—	2 ♥	3 ♣	—
—	3 ♥	—	4 ♥
—	—	Double	All pass

Result: 10 tricks made

This is a not untypical example of early Blue Book bridge. Note how Jo Culbertson drags the reluctant English, both of whom have passed on the first round, by the scruffs of their necks into a cast-iron game, which neither wishes to bid. Then, to add a bonus to generosity, she doubles them.

And this was the match which made the Culbertsons famous!

3

Lenz, Lunacy and Murder

When Culbertson had left the United States a few weeks before, he was almost unknown. Thanks to Buller and the *Blue Book* he returned famous. When his ship docked it was literally overrun. For the first and only time in his life he had had enough of the limelight and, escaping through the luggage gangway, he was smuggled through Customs.

The excitement at the dock was no ephemeral demonstration, it turned out to be an announcement that Contract had finally and permanently arrived. Why a card game should so effectually capture the popular imagination, not as a passing craze but as an institution, is an insoluble enigma. Culbertson did not try to solve it. In January 1959 the *Bridge Magazine* was able to announce that it sold in sixty-six countries which it listed, including such exotic and far-flung places as Java, Iceland and Indo-China.

While this was in the future, Ely's first task was to found an industry in the United States, with himself in complete control. Everything else would follow. He neglected nothing that could further this object. Building up the news value of Contract he tied up with Jack Wheeler, President of the Bell Syndicate, he became associated with N.B.C., and R.K.O., as well as various agencies, editors and sportscasters.

There were nationwide lecture tours by himself and Jo. He formed a company, The Culbertson National Studios Inc., through which he perfected his teacher organization into a closely knit body of 4,000, with over a million pupils. By September 1931 it had moved to the General Western Building on Lexington Avenue where on a $15,000 a month payroll a staff answered, classified and filed letters, dealt with books and newspaper articles, adopted and adapted ideas, and indeed did all the work incidental to a well-run Bridge laboratory.

Jo had written a summary of the *Blue Book,* which was to net $250,000. Some weeks the sales of the *Blue Book* reached $10,000, and it was to sell eventually 1,300,000 copies.

The Buller match was certainly played for greater stakes than Almacks had seen even in the days of its deepest play.

Now all this, though hectic, was pleasant, but soon a cacophony of screams of pain and rage was heard from the jungle inhabited by the other Bridge authorities who had hitherto roamed at will, but were suddenly faced with extermination. With the rise of Contract, and the eclipse of Auction, each had produced a system, some good, some bad, some indifferent, but all gratifying to Culbertson to whom a bewildered public turned, partly because his system had proved successful, and partly because it was so widely played that they decided it was easier to speak one language than fifty.

Faced with the common threat the pundits did the only possible thing: they made peace. Having decided that there was plunder and to spare for all, the twelve leading authorities banded together. In a self-denying ordinance Lenz, Whitehead, Work, Shephard *et al.* threw their systems into a collective melting pot, and in March 1931 they announced the birth of the Official System of Contract Bridge. The credit for this diabolically clever designation belongs to their business manager, F. D. Courtenay, a smooth operator. The astuteness was that it had the manifest authority and imprimatur of the old established aristocracy of Bridge, and seemingly represented the distillation of its collective wisdom and experience.

For a couple of months they allowed Mr. Culbertson to ponder this new development, which he did with a certain amount of unhappiness. When they considered the time was ripe, and the victim in a suitable frame of mind, they made generous overtures to usher in the prosperous days of peace for all—or so they fondly thought!

One sunny and propitious morning in the month of May, the blandly urbane Mr. Courtenay was ceremoniously ushered into Culbertson's office. After a few well-chosen pleasantries, he came straight to his point. He was authorized, he said, by his principals to invite Mr. Culbertson and his organization to join them in their mutual interests. Just as pleasantly Culbertson inquired innocently how many principals he represented.

"The twelve leading authorities in the United States," he was informed.

"Mr. Courtenay," was the regretful reply, "I am a believer in luck and that would make me number thirteen. There is, I am afraid, only room for one."

A declaration of war has never been couched more suavely.

Ely Culbertson was under no illusion. This second great crisis coming so soon after the first was by far the more important. If the Buller contest was the foundation of his fortunes, defeat this time would be their ruination; as he had implied to Courtenay, there could be no compromise between the Official System and his. Only one could survive, and time was on the side of the enemy. It was true that money was pouring in, but as fast as it arrived it was injected into his expanding enterprises. Paradoxically, he had no money himself beyond expenses, and he was painfully aware that the damming of the life stream of dollars for even a few weeks could strangle his credit and his sales, and bring down the edifice he had worked so hard to consolidate.

His strategy, then, was to bring about a showdown between the Culbertson and Official Systems as soon as possible. His tactics were masterly.

The Official System was personified in Lenz, its moving spirit, and foremost protagonist. For Culbertson he was the natural and foreordained antagonist, and he concentrated all his batteries on him. As a publicity maneuver he could not have picked a more rewarding target.

Sidney Horatio Lenz was no less colorful a character than Culbertson himself. Son of a rich father, at the university he had had a spectacular career, both academic and sporting. He then decided to make some money and having done so to the tune of several millions as a timber tycoon, he retired from business at the age of thirty-five. He certainly did not retire from anything else. The president of the Magicians' Circle, his friend Houdini, said he thanked heaven Lenz had never turned professional. For years he was draughts and table-tennis champion of America. He played tennis on nearly equal terms with the great Tilden, and golf with such performers as Francis Ouimet and Walter Hagen. He is reputed to have helped Harry Greb for his winning championship fight with Mickey Walker. He was also a champion bowls player, and Capablanca was always glad to play chess with him. He was undoubtedly the best all-round card player in the world, and when he learned Bridge from some Indian Army officers he wrote *Lenz on Bridge,* still a classic of the older game. Add to this the fact that he was an indefatigable globe trotter, who spoke six languages fluently and could be understood in about thirty others, and you arrive at the portrait of a fabulous character no romantic novelist would have the nerve to invent.

Lenz must have cursed the day he identified the Official System with himself. Despite his accomplishments he was an unassuming man. He had nothing to gain by entering the lists with anyone, nor did he want to. What he had not reckoned on was that Culbertson stood to lose everything, and was determined at all costs to survive; to do so he simply had to establish his system by victory in battle. Everything was now subordinated to that single overriding object.

When the date was finally fixed the contest was universally labelled "The Bridge Battle of the Century," and for once the public was not deceived. This time the usual pretentious title was justified, for from this match emerged the pattern of Contract Bridge as we know it today. This does not imply that Contract would not have developed and survived, but had the outcome of the match been different so would have been its evolution.

With consummate finesse Culbertson went to work. Through the *Bridge World,* radio and press he played a series of variations on the three main themes which he decided would best serve to capture his audience. These were Sympathy, Self-Interest, and Dramatic Interest. As to the first, he had chosen Jo as his partner mainly because she was the better player, and had helped in formulating his system. But as his wife, she was an even greater asset for he could present an image of twelve jealous men combining against a young married couple fighting alone. From the first he had every housewife in the nation on his side. The second variation, self-interest, lay in the battle of the Systems. The public wanted the best, and were persuaded that the winning side would be that which played the better system. With this in mind he was at pains to pay tribute to Lenz, the card player, while sympathizing with his misfortune in being committed to play the Official System which, of course, gave him no chance of victory.

As to dramatic interest, knowing the rabid gusto engendered by a grudge match, Culbertson baited his opponent relentlessly. In the classic legal phrase he used every weapon of hatred, odium, ridicule and contempt available to him and he had a well-stocked armory. Eventually, goaded beyond the limits of endurance, with a punch-drunk public insisting on the contest, Lenz capitulated and nominated Oswald Jacoby as his partner. That was in November 1931, and from then until the end of the match no such extravaganza as ensued had ever been seen before, and will assuredly never be seen again. Even at this distance, looking back it has an aura of pure surrealistic fantasy through which the figures move as in a chimera imagined by Lewis Carroll and designed by Gustave Doré.

Reading the contemporary newspapers one becomes aware that two important events occurred in the United States that month. There was a presidential election, and the signing of the contract for the Lenz-Culbertson match.

The signing atracted more publicity than any world champion prizefighter had ever seen. Even so staid a journal as the *New York Times* headlined it as "the sporting event of the year." The contract was drawn up by a leading firm of New York lawyers, and ran to eleven closely typewritten pages and seventy-two clauses. To accommodate the press, photographers, and what looked like the rest of the population of New York, the principals executed this impressive document in the Waldorf-Astoria, which got a slight foretaste of what was to come the following month.

The most important terms were: *(a)* One hundred and fifty rubbers were to be played; *(b)* each partnership to play its own system; *(c)* bets and stakes by arrangement; *(d)* provision for a referee, observers, stenographers, recorders and conditions of play generally; (e) at least seventy-five rubbers to be played with the designated partner, otherwise any other partner could be chosen: Lenz and Culbertson had to play throughout; *(f)* the match to begin on December 8 at the Chatham and proceed for the latter half at the Waldorf. Apart from a short Christmas break, play was to be continuous in two daily sessions.

Culbertson bet $10,000 with Lenz and Jacoby at odds varying from 5 to 1 to 3 to 1 on himself; he made these odds available to sundry other sporting types. Each player announced that the proceeds of stakes and bets would go to charity. This fooled nobody. Charity might benefit to the extent of a few thousand dollars, but the big bet, as the *Herald Tribune* pointed out, was for the control of the entire Bridge industry.

The remaining weeks before the match were feverish. Every day the papers came out with some new extravagance. The interest was hardly less in London where it was the main news story also, to the eloquent fury of Buller whose British Bridge had taken a vertiginous dive since the previous year.

Publicity burgeoned.

One day Damon Runyon announced through his column that

he would pick a team from his associates on Broadway and play Culbertson for $25 a point any time he liked. At the then scale of scoring, that would have made the bonus for a vulnerable Grand Slam worth $56,250. The Master replied with dignity that he had no desire to rob Mr. Runyon and his friends of their Christmas toys.

In downtown Brooklyn two barbers, Ed Jansen and Johnnie Ditzler, began a marathon crap game to establish the superiority of the "African Twist" or the "Direct Throw." The late results were posted in their shop windows.

The public loved it.

In the meantime, Culbertson had got down to business. The Chatham, hitherto a caravansery of quiet and luxurious distinction, was taken over by a horde of madmen who proceeded with purposeful passion to take it apart at the seams. Associated Press laid twenty-four cables, and Western Union and Postal Telegraph assigned eight representatives, working twenty-four hours round the clock, to send reports to all parts of the world. Over a hundred reporters were on duty. The newsreel and radio boys arrived, and cameras, microphones and kleig lamps were set up.

The players, and those officials who had access, were screened off from distraction in a chastely appointed room. Deliberately, however, cracks were left in the screen through which the curious could peek and hear. The next month exhibited the edifying spectacle of bank-presidents and publishers, bishops and actresses, the reverent and the profane, queueing in a continuous stream to squint in acute discomfort at a game of Contract Bridge. It is pleasant to record that during the whole match it was necessary only once to eject an uninvited peeker.

At 7 P.M., on Tuesday December 8, 1931, one hour before play began, the machine went into action. The principals were introduced, interviewed and photographed. The names of the officials were announced. These consisted, in order of unimportance, of stenographers, who recorded every word, scorers, observers (Colonel J. J. Walshe, correspondent of *The Times,* and Yarborough of the *Sunday Times* represented England), and two honorary referees, one appointed by each team.

The umpire and final arbiter, resplendent in his undress uniform, was Lieutenant Alfred M. Gruenther of West Point, who some years later discharged a somewhat less arduous duty when as a five-star general he was Commander-in-Chief of the Allied Forces in Europe.

No pack of cards could be used twice, and they were all shuffled and resealed in conditions of military security by selected cadets at West Point whence the Army delivered them. Over a thousand packs were to be used.

Lieutenant Gruenther broke the seal on the first pack, and the Battle of the Century had begun.

One of Culbertson's apothegms was, "I play men, not cards." He certainly put precept into practice as far as his opponents were concerned. Not once did he turn up on time, although he lived at the Chatham. He soon spotted that the keen-witted Lenz liked to bid and play as quickly as possible, which at Bridge means as quickly as your opponents will let you. On one occasion Ely delayed so long in playing a card that the exasperated Lenz, although he was declarer, exploded, "I am going out to a speakeasy for a drink," and did!

Lenz had other troubles, notably that after every hand Culbertson, and later Jacoby—not to be outdone—sent out conflicting comments to the press. During these interludes the martyred Lenz was ostentatiously engrossed in a book.

The limit was reached shortly before Christmas. The first hand had hardly been dealt when around the screen to kiss goodnight, and fetchingly attired in blue silk nighties, toddled Miss Joyce Culbertson, aged four, and her small brother Bruce, affectionately called "Jump Bid." Their fond parents saw them photographed and interviewed by the delighted press and Hollywood boys. Jacoby observed that so far they were the first to talk any sense during the match.

That night for the first and only time in his life Lenz misplayed a hand because he forgot what was trumps. He could console himself that *that* got headlines as well.

Jo announced that she was taking a break to do her shopping and be with the children. There was no objection, but the papers got another story.

There were repeated recriminations that each side had departed from its announced system. The *Herald Tribune* said, "Both teams originated enough new bids to inaugurate a new brand of game."

Before Lieutenant Gruenther handed out the first pack on December 18 Culbertson politely remarked to his opponent, "If you want to make me happy, tell me right now you are playing the Culbertson System."

"I don't know what is the Culbertson System," Lenz replied, "and I don't think you do either."

"But, Sidney, I have already sent you two copies of the *Blue Book*."

The irrepressible Jacoby saved the situation. "I wish you'd send me two more, Ely. I have a table at home with a short leg."

At first, due mainly to superior cards, Lenz had gone ahead, but the self-possessed Culbertson always exuded confidence in his nightly broadcasts and daily articles. When the pendulum began to swing in his direction the excitement waxed.

Westbrook Pegler, who interviewed him for the *Chicago Tribune* wrote:

> Now that Bridge has passed prize-fighting in popular interest, I asked him for a comment. He told me that to make the best of both games he would challenge Tunney and me, if he could have Dempsey.

"Are your published statistics of Bridge players accurate, Mr. Culbertson?"

"Well, we must leave out the kids, the ignorant and the insane."

"How many does that leave?"

"Let's talk of something else."

"O.K., who picks up the tab for all this?"

"This is a very high class game, and a very high class hotel."

"Sure, but Tex Rickard built his own stadium. What's your angle? You say you don't get a dime. It isn't because you love humanity, is it?"

"Well, I figure to make about $500,000."

Neither Mr. Pegler nor anyone else could suspect that the game would, in fact, bring him a great deal more than that. Even the usually accurate *New York Times* was short of the mark when, on the seventh, it put the prize as being the entire Bridge-publishing business in the U.S.A.

After Christmas, on December 28, the game continued at the Waldorf-Astoria. Jo had resumed in place of Teddy Lightner who had substituted, and the pressure was really on Lenz, whose team was now 17,090 points behind. That very night, despite the lady's soothing presence, the strain proved too much.

Jacoby, the youngest of the four, had from time to time displayed a penchant for "psychic," or bluff calls—bids designed to mislead the opponents. Unfortunately they can have the boomerang effect of misleading a partner, which can be expensive. Usually Jacoby's efforts were well-timed and successful, but had done little to ease the electric atmosphere. On this night he overcalled an opening bid of Jo's with One No Trump without as much as a face card in his hand. The Culbertsons ignored the call and bid and made game in No Trumps. Although the call, which was fatuous, had done no harm, Lenz blew up and accused Jacoby of making any partnership understanding impossible.

Jacoby turned pale with anger but played out the rest of the rubber in silence. When it was over he stood up and said: "Well, that's it. I'm through."

It was now five minutes to twelve, and Gruenther pointed out that under the terms of the match a fresh rubber must be played if the last one finished before midnight.

"Not with me it won't."

Eventually Jacoby reluctantly agreed to continue, but after it was played he shook hands with his partner and repeated his resignation; later that night he gave it in writing. He had played 108 rubbers.

Jacoby was replaced by Commander Winfield Liggett, Jr., of the United States Navy, and the marathon continued. From being at one time 20,220 behind, Lenz retrieved some ground. But his opponent was so confident that after the New Year he allowed his friends Howard Schenken and "Mike" Gottlieb to partner him.

Possibly the public expected a miracle, but at any rate there was no slackening of activity around the Waldorf.

Ring Lardner described hordes of hotel servants in livery and gold braid bleating "page Culbertson" with metronomic regularity; Lenz muttered it in his nightmares he said. Waddles of tiptoeing dowagers shooed at each other in the lush corridors. An entire wing of the huge hotel was taken over, at one end of which Lenz, who lived there, had his headquarters. Culbertson had encamped as far away as possible, complete with day and night nursery for Baby Joyce and "Jump Bid." Both establishments were cordoned off from profane eyes with velvet ropes. "A circus atmosphere clung to the Bridge marathon like the scent of beer to a speakeasy. You could write your testimonial in cigarette smoke." (Ring Lardner in the *New York Herald Tribune,* December 1931.)

When the players sat down for the final session Culbertson, who was over ten thousand points ahead, without looking at his cards said "No Bid. I cannot lose, so I am not going to bid at all tonight."

The referee was nonplussed; there was no rule against this. Mrs. C. soon stopped the nonsense.

"I think that's absolutely ridiculous, Ely. Look at your cards at once."

That was the end of that.

The final hand was a game called and made by Jo. When she played the last card of the match for an overall victory by 8,980 points, pandemonium broke out. The barriers were down.

One reporter described "a milling throng of stiff white shirts and ermine coats rubbing shoulders with the plain and garden kibitzers."

True to form, Culbertson somehow broke through them to the Associated Press. He broadcast the glad tidings on the coast to coast radio network. History records his peroration: "The grand finale was one of those freaks which, like a rare comet in the firmament, gravitates in the outermost limits of distribution."

This was his way of describing the last hand which, in fact, depended on Jo's taking a finesse successfully. However, it was a typical piece of rhetorical flatulence on which to wind up the broadcast and the match.

Lenz, congratulating Jo, said he never wished to play against a pleasanter opponent. Speeches all round and toasts anticipated the abolition of Prohibition but, as the papers reported, there were no handshakes between Mr. Lenz and Mr. Culbertson.

There was a tidal wave of reporters.

"Yes, I bet Lenz five to one."

"Yes, all bets go to charity."

"I bet Chico Marx three hundred to a hundred, but I didn't get his check yet."

Lenz's comment was "Luck decided it."

Nobody listened to him.

There was an interruption of the revelry from a telegraph operator: "The London papers are holding up their last editions."

The final score was flashed to them.

Culbertson awoke on January 8, 1932 "broke, but happy." He was broke because before the match the sales of the *Blue Book* and *Summary* had been dwindling; during it, pending the result, hardly a copy sold. From now on they skyrocketed up and ever up beyond his most extravagant hopes.

The publicity was fantastic. The newspapers, as the *New York Times* put it, saw bridge as a major sport in the same class as football, baseball, and prizefighting. The *Herald Tribune* announced it had now put off its swaddling clothes and was big business. In American papers over two million words were written on the Lenz match, more than on the Lindbergh flight.

Before the match Culbertson had engaged a press-cutting agency and forgotten about it. He remembered when the manager of the Chatham told him there was no more storage room. At the same time there was a bill for $2,150 due to the agency.

In a speech to the press, Heywood Broun said he was looking for Utopia, and had no doubt the Culbertson System would be played there. Ely had to recruit more staff to deal with the flood of correspondence, telephone messages, and callers. As he said himself, "All hell had broken out." Three "whodunits," with bridge as a background, were published, and Hollywood cashed in with a film, *Grand Slam,* starring Loretta Young and Paul Lukas. There was an inundation of business offers and suggestions for endorsements, at some of which Jo blushed.

One day a prosperous looking and persuasive gentleman arrived with a proposition. It transpired he was the representative of a leading manufacturer of toilet paper. His suggestion was that some feature of the Culbertson System be displayed on his wares. He could guarantee vast publicity.

Culbertson's reaction was immediate: "Look, my friend, every hour of every day thousands of people do the most shocking things to my system, but I'll be damned if I'll let them do that!"

Another day a trio of impressive and obviously affluent businessmen were shown in. They were the chairman, secretary, and a member of the board of one of America's biggest whiskey distillers. Culbertson sat up, and they sat down.

They had taken the liberty, they said, of bringing two samples of whiskey. One was of a famous Scotch brand, the other a synthetic product of their own. They hoped Mr. Culbertson would not be insulted if they offered him a token $10,000 for endorsing it. Of course, it would be based on an honest test.

The unresisting, but astonished, Culbertson was blindfolded

and given two glasses. He sipped each, the handkerchief was removed.

"Well?" The three gentlemen smiled encouragingly.

"The second one."

The blindfold was replaced. That was only a trial, they explained, and went through the same ritual with the whiskey glasses.

"Now, which do you prefer?"

Culbertson thought hard. After all, ten thousand was not bad. He tried again, and took a deep breath. "The first one," he said firmly.

There was a pregnant pause. "Well, Mr. Culbertson, we will probably get in touch with you."

As he was closing the door behind them, he heard the secretary remark pungently. "I don't know what sort of a system has been invented by a guy who can't even win on a three to one shot."

His relations with Chesterfield cigarettes and Wrigley's chewing gum were more lucrative. For the former he prepared a booklet which was distributed free with each packet of cigarettes to more than 3,000,000 purchasers. Wrigley's printed some of his system on their wrappers.

There were radio contracts for himself and Jo; and for the R.K.O. film studios in Hollywood, starring with Anita Louise and Julie Haydon, they made a series of six short films, which did not make cinematic history, but did make nice money.

The teachers now numbered more than 10,000, his articles were syndicated in more than 150 American and foreign newspapers, Jo's in those belonging to the Hearst organization. At the same time *Blue Book* and *Summary* sales soared. They were translated into twelve languages, and printed in Braille; they found their way into lumber camps, hospitals and, appropriately, asylums. It is a fact that there was a near riot in Sing-Sing between two student groups who disagreed as to the correct system bid.

Ely was now a millionaire, but there was still work to do

before he would let himself sit back, although at the beginning of the year 1933 he could look back on his achievements with a sense of fulfilment. Except for a few unimportant partisan pockets he had conquered not only America but his principles were gaining acceptance all over the world. In three years he had transmuted Contract Bridge from a recreation for the few into an addiction for the million; he had made it an industry, and in England that year it was to become a spectator sport.

There had been one extraordinary piece of luck, which neither then nor ever did he acknowledge, but which fomented such a feverish interest in Contract Bridge as to ensure for his war with Lenz publicity beyond the wildest expectation.

This was the unforgettable Murder Trial of Myrtle Bennett, who had shot her husband over a game of bridge.

It will be remembered that in March 1931 the birth of the Official System was announced with a trumpet blast. The moment was well chosen, for that very month the Bennett trial had built up, or rather soared, to a climax unprecedented in the legal annals of even that stormy era.

On the night of September 29, 1929, in their apartment in the fashionable south-side of Kansas City, John G. Bennett distributed the cards in a deal that became as legendary as the fateful Dead Man's Hand of Wild Bill Hickok. Neither the locale, the players nor the stakes—one-tenth of a cent per point—appeared to be laden with doom, yet, so it proved.

Playing in a rubber with their friends, Charlie and Mayme Hofman, Mr. Bennett opened the bidding with One Spade, and over Mr. Hofman's intervention of Two Diamonds, Myrtle contracted for Four Spades. John Bennett's performance did not match his wife's ambition, and he failed in his contract by one trick. Thereupon, Myrtle, according to subsequent evidence, not only characterized her husband as a "bum bridge player," but was heard to comment unfavorably upon his parentage. John G. in turn spoke severely about Myrtle's bidding, and about her I.Q. generally. To emphasize his reprimand he slapped her twice on the cheeks. Myrtle, sensible of her duties as hostess observed that "only a cur would strike his wife in the presence of company." Having made this incontestable point of etiquette, and feeling the conversation had lasted too long anyway, she burst into tears, and rushed from the room.

That tears are not the only weapon available to the slighted spouse she proved conclusively and dramatically upon her speedy return. Armed with a Browning automatic, with an accuracy of aim wholly admirable in her distraught condition, she shot Mr. Bennett dead.

The ensuing trial began in February 1931 and continued well into the following month. There were no tales from Hofman, both husband and wife being too shocked to remember details. The highlight, in fact, was the address of junior counsel for the defence. Above the sobbing of the accused, her mother, and the foreman of the jury, not to mention the manly emotion of his learned colleague, Senator James A. Reid, he could hardly be heard as he assured the Court that, "I know what Jack Bennett would want me to do. If he were here today, he would order me to protect the wife he loved, and give solace to the old mother-in-law he loved."

Without, presumably, being too technical as to the reason for Jack's absence, the jury found not Justifiable Homicide as might have been expected, but Accidental Death. Myrtle was acquitted.

There is an epilogue to this doleful tale, for it was now the turn of the insurance company to give way to manly emotion when it discovered that it owed the bereaved widow $30,000, for which sum the late Mr. Bennett had thoughtfully insured his life with them against death by accident.

Culbertson is quoted as having commented, "Poor Bennett, if he had only played the Culbertson System he would have saved his life!"

THE BATTLE OF THE CENTURY
Culbertson v Lenz

DEALER EAST.
LOVE ALL.

NORTH
Sidney Lenz
♠ Q J 9 5 3
♥ Q J 6 3
♦ J 7 2
♣ 8

WEST
Ely Culbertson
♠ A K 8
♥ A K 4
♦ 10 8 5
♣ 9 6 4 2

EAST
Jo Culbertson
♠ 10 6 2
♥ —
♦ A K Q 9 6 4 3
♣ A 5 3

SOUTH
Commander Liggett
♠ 7 4
♥ 10 9 8 7 5 2
♦ —
♣ K Q J 10 7

East	South	West	North
1 ♦	1 ♥	2 N T	No
3 N T	All Pass		

Result: 12 tricks made.

A fair example of the slam bidding of the period, and of the Battle of the Century in particular. Comment is superfluous.

THE BATTLE OF THE CENTURY
Culbertson v Lenz

DEALER NORTH.

LOVE ALL.

NORTH
Sidney Lenz
- ♠ 9 8 6 2
- ♥ A 8 3 2
- ♦ J 6 3
- ♣ 10 3

WEST
Ely Culbertson
- ♠ Q 5 4
- ♥ J
- ♦ 7 5 4
- ♣ A K Q 9 8 6

EAST
Jo Culbertson
- ♠ A 10
- ♥ Q 10 6 5
- ♦ K Q 9 8 3
- ♣ 7 2

SOUTH
Oswald Jacoby
- ♠ K J 7 3
- ♥ K 9 7 4
- ♦ A 10
- ♣ J 5 4

North	East	South	West
No	No	1 ♠	1 N T
2 ♠	2 N T	All Pass	

Result: 8 tricks made

Another prime example of the standard in this match. Only
Jacoby bid correctly. Ely successfully psyched himself out of
3 N T, into which, for some reason, Jo, having passed, refused
to raise him. For no ascertainable reason, having obtained a
spade lead, Ely refrained from making 9 tricks!

THE BENNETT MURDER HAND
Kansas City, September 1929

SOUTH DEALS.

N.S. VULNERABLE.

NORTH

Myrtle

♠ A 10 6 3
♥ 10 8 5
♦ 4
♣ A 9 8 4 2

WEST

Charlie

♠ Q 7 2
♥ A J 3
♦ A Q 10 9 2
♣ J 6

EAST

Mayme

♠ 4
♥ Q 9 4
♦ K J 7 6 3
♣ Q 7 5 3

SOUTH

John G.

♠ K J 9 8 5
♥ K 7 6 2
♦ 8 5
♣ K 10

South	West	North	East
1 ♠	2 ♦	4 ♠	All pass

Result: down 1

Charlie led the Ace of Diamonds and shifted to the Knave of Clubs. If John G. had won that with the King, played the King of Spades, and made the percentage play of finessing the ten of trumps, then played the Ace of Spades, Ace of Clubs, and ran clubs through Mayme, he could have re-entered dummy with a ruff, discarded two losing hearts, thereby saving the con-

44

going on this time, he set to work producing a show in London which would finally establish Contract as a major spectator sport. He had always held it as a cherished certainty that people would not only read avidly about the game and play it, but they would also come to see it. Up to now, he had never had a chance to prove his conviction. Indeed this was his only lingering regret about his match with Lenz.

The great and pressing problem was where in London could be staged the match on the spectacular scale he envisaged. There could be no question of a public auditorium because the players must have privacy, silence, and freedom from distraction. On the other hand, it was necessary that every bid, and every play, be followed closely by an audience of thousands. If humanly possible, the players should also be seen. Even television, were it available, could not supply the answer, but the acumen of Gordon Selfridge did!

Selfridge had achieved his dominant position on the Napoleonic canon that the impossible takes just a little longer to accomplish than the improbable. When, therefore, the uncertain promoters of the match approached him with their troubles, he sent them rejoicing on their way. He had never seen a hand of Bridge in his life, but he did see that here was an opportunity not to be missed, and he placed at their disposal the entire resources of his vast and famous emporium. Thanks to this inspiration, and the genius of Culbertson as a showman, he had brought off as brilliant and farseeing a *coup* as a lifetime of successful enterprise records.

Difficulties vanished. Two large rooms for play were set aside and furnished. The furniture included among its trappings green plush ropes enclosing a ring in which the players sat on red upholstered chairs at a Sheraton card table, the walls being tastefully draped in beige and white. The sedative effect of this monastic austerity was no doubt designed, as Dr. Johnson would have said, wonderfully to concentrate the mind.

If the arena itself was faintly reminiscent of the Brighton Pavilion, the balance was redressed outside. Here the Palm

49

Court of Selfridges, languid betimes with the whispering of
lotus-eaters and the sob of teatime violins, was now abandoned
to the exactions of ballyhoo and Ely Culbertson. Along one
wall had been erected a huge electronic scoreboard, picked out
in colored lights. This contrivance was so constructed that all
spectators would see what cards were held by each player, and
could follow step by step the bidding and the play of every
card. There was also a space for the result of every board, and
for the current score. Nor was this all, for by an ingenious
system of periscopes, and an even more ingenious arrangement
of refracting mirrors, the actual contestants themselves could
be seen playing at the table. There was at all times a commentator standing at the scoreboard—himself an expert—who gave
a running explanation of the bids and plays as they were made,
and commented on each hand when it was finished.

The result of this *tour de force* of organization was that the
spectators knew more of the progress of the match than did
the actual participants, and had the additional advantage of
being able to see how the British and American teams dealt
respectively with the more difficult and exciting hands.

Nothing like it had ever been attempted before but the
gamble, if gamble it was, succeeded in a way that left even
Fleet Street groping for adjectives. For the six days of the
match over 27,000 people succeeded in watching it in
Selfridges, and so many more were left outside that the police,
unable to cope, were compelled to divert the traffic.

The newspapers would have splashed the match in any
event. As it was, they did a great deal more. Culbertson had a
retainer from the *News Chronicle* to cover the Championship
day by day, and the *Daily Mail* had a similar arrangement with
Beasley. Apart from that, both papers treated the match as front
page news with banner headlines and the *Daily Express,* which
had been scooped, had to play along in a lower key.

No single detail was overlooked by Fleet Street, and top reporters, male and female, were assigned. On three days car-
toons appeared by Tom Webster, and on the opening day the

News Chronicle came out with the faces of the Americans as playing cards, Jo being the Queen of Hearts. *The Times* was more restrained. With that majestic philosophy that what should not exist does not exist it allotted an inch and a half to an announcement of the match. Prominently featured for the rest of the week on its sporting page was a blow-by-blow account of the finals of the inter-county chess championship. It is only fair to record that it did open its correspondence columns to some military gentlemen who wrote deploring, but not mentioning, the affair at Selfridges, of which they must have heard by chance.

On the evening of July 17 it was apparent that quite a few other people had also heard, because the teams themselves had difficulty in getting to their places through the crowds. When they did it was observed that Lady Rhodes of the British team was dressed in diaphanous green, while Jo appeared in a confection of light check and carrying a bouquet of carnations.

The British team apart from Beasley was Lady Rhodes, Percy Tabbush, Sir Guy Domville, and Graham Mathieson.

The task that Culbertson had set himself for the ensuing week almost defies belief, and yet, in the sacred cause of publicity, he accomplished it. Not only had he to write his daily column for the *News Chronicle,* but he had to prepare two midnight broadcasts to New York, where the five hour time lag ensured peak listening. In addition, and in conjunction with the *News Chronicle* he was to have a complete book of the match written, published and on sale by 2 P.M. the following Monday.

This unexampled feat of publication entailed a volume of 400 pages, including all three hundred hands with comments by himself, pen portraits of the players, and a foreword by Hubert Phillips. As far as is known, this set up a record which has never since been approached in publishing history. It meant also that Culbertson had hardly any sleep during the week, and none at all for the last two days and nights.

From the very beginning an atmosphere of fourth-dimensional insanity enveloped the World Championship. When the first board was dealt, Culbertson picked up his hand and demanded:

"What are these things supposed to be. It's not my birthday!"

The explanation was that the unfortunate "Pops" Beasley had decided to show the Americans that the phlegmatic British had a fitting sense of occasion also. He had had made at appalling expense playing cards of somewhat surrealistic design which were to be distributed as souvenirs after the match. Culbertson refused to touch them: he said they were bad for his stomach.

Play began at last, but not for long. The next crisis was over the lighting. This had been installed by the best electricians in London who had the intricate job of satisfying the requirements of the periscopes, the mirrors, and the players. Ely's eyes, which could ordinarily distinguish the Ace of Spades in a London fog, were unequal to this handicap so the lights were changed.

After these two well-timed strokes of gamesmanship one could hardly blame Beasley if he had been put off his game. On the contrary, however, his team played like angels, and after the first encounter they led by a couple of thousand points. Culbertson sent a cable to New York ordering the Stars and Stripes to fly at half-mast over his club.

As a result of the home team's unexpected lead, which lasted for two days, Selfridges became the London Mecca. Royalty arrived, incognito it is true, but very regal. Poor Ely broadcasting later to the United States nearly burst a blood vessel observing the protocol of secrecy. The Duke of Roxburghe had reserved a seat beside the players, which he occupied for the entire week. The Royal Physician, Lord Moynihan, was there. So too were the Earl and Countess of Scarsdale with the Duke of Manchester—whose daughter, Lady Mary Montagu, was an official scorer. Republican hearts rejoiced, the last aristocratic bastions had fallen.

From the British point of view it was all too good to last. The tide began to turn, and on the third day the Stop Press column disclosed the ominous news that England was only 420 ahead. As this represented less than one vulnerable game the writing was on the wall.

On Wednesday, July 19, everything happened at once. Graham Mathieson of the English team almost fell to his death through a glass roof, and was rescued hanging by one hand to an iron girder over a forty-foot drop.

His teammates in the card room were also holding on with difficulty. As often happens, the cards did not give much scope to either team, but as the match progressed, as if to reflect the excitement of the spectators, they began to show signs of skittishness. Big hands began to abound, and the superior American technique of dealing with them became apparent.

The new 4-5 No Trump convention proved its worth, and the result was disastrous for the English. Points began to pour back, and at the end of the day the visitors commanded a good lead which they increased steadily until the end of the match.

In his broadcast their captain informed millions of his compatriots that the English became "bogged down in the treacherous swamp of the slam-zone," and in his daily report he wrote modestly that "the Culbertson system worked with the deadly accuracy of machine gun fire." The suggestion in Tom Webster's cartoon, that England should pick Larwood, the demon fast bowler of body-line fame, to counteract these lethal methods would hardly have proved an adequate defence.

The papers were now enjoying themselves and on Thursday, July 20, the headlines came out in full luxuriance. STREET CROWDS CHEER SCORES; SCORERS MOBBED BY EXCITED SPECTATORS; "SHEER TRAGEDY FOR ENGLAND" SAYS BEASLEY. This last pronouncement referred to a fatal hand played by his partner the previous day, which still echoes down the halls of time.

Sir Guy Domville, who had hitherto proved the steadiest of the English team, came into the Auction with a bid of Two

Hearts vulnerable, although Culbertson had opened the bidding with One Heart. Domville's bid, to his amazement, was passed out. His partner held two small hearts, and his only trump was the Ace; it was also the only trick he made. Seven down vulnerable in those days was 1,750 points, a catastrophe which was not mitigated by the fact that there was no slam to be made by the opponents. There can be no question that Beasley was in the wrong. Very much later he was forced to acknowledge this. The following day, however, in the *Daily Mail* his summing up was terse and to the point. "It was a lunatic call of my partner's." The opposing captain was more charitable, as he could afford to be; in the *News Chronicle* he said, "It takes an expert to go down seven tricks!"

By Friday the crowds in Oxford Street had become a major problem. Inside Selfridges it was impossible to get a seat for hours before the play began. When Culbertson arrived his usual, imperturbable *sang-froid* showed signs of wearing thin. Whether this was due to overwork or the previous day's thunder-stealing act of Beasley-Domville we can never know. At any rate, he announced immediately, "I am not going to play with my wife. I can't stand any partner more than three days running."

In an earlier handout he informed the press, "I only play my very best in partnership with my brilliant wife."

Having looked balefully at his apprehensive teammates he then proclaimed, "And, furthermore, I will not play with Lightner. Lightner makes me sick." To guard against this nauseating influence he poured himself some indigestion mixture which he swallowed.

This Draconian method of team selection left only "Mike" Gottlieb who duly took his place opposite the master, whereupon Jo and Lightner proceeded to play the best Bridge of the entire match.

The overture, which should have been scored by Tchaikovsky, provided an appropriate introduction to the day's events. The proceedings became infected with a kind of constrained delirium until the tension became intolerable. Something had to give, and it turned out to be Lady Mary Montagu who fell off her chair and broke her arm. Her ducal father was not unnerved, and for the rest of the match carried out her duties as scorer in a manner which did great credit to his moral fiber.

It is pleasant to record that while the *Daily Express* headlined "The Most Amazing Bridge Match Ever Played," no untoward incident from the finals of the inter-county chess match was reported in *The Times*.

The final day for the public should have been an anticlimax, but it was not. The fact that short of a miracle England could not win did not deter them from thronging in. And if there is one thing that gives a crowd more pleasure than seeing an expert play brilliantly, it is to see him making an ass of himself. Both types of enjoyment were afforded on the final day.

First, Culbertson played a hand in Two Clubs and made thirteen tricks. This compares roughly with missing a two-inch putt in golf, and the spectators were duly appreciative. At the end of the match Lady Rhodes, who had played excellently, found herself in a small slam which Culbertson incontinently doubled. Undaunted she redoubled and made her contract with aplomb. The cheers could be heard in Piccadilly!

For Britain, however, these fireworks had come too late to affect the final tally which read: For England: 93,180. For U.S.A.: 104,080. The Americans had won by 10,900 points.

Next came the unparalleled feat of producing the Book of the Match. The championship finished at 2 A.M., on Sunday morning, July 23. Culbertson bet an incredulous English friend £100 that the book would be on sale in the London stores at 2 P.M. the following day, thirty-six hours later. It was.

It is difficult to apportion the credit because everyone connected with the extraordinary undertaking is entitled to it. It was earned particularly by Culbertson himself, who had read the galley proofs, made comments on every hand, and in addition broadcast twice to the United States, all in the course of playing an arduous match. Perhaps the best tribute came from the chairman of De la Rue when, in the course of a letter to the *News Chronicle,* congratulating it and the printers, Messrs. James Truscott, he said that after a lifetime of printing and publishing he would not have believed that such a fantastic achievement was possible.

Insurance companies are ruefully aware of certain types who are known to them as accident-prone. For no particular reason they press the wrong button, walk through plate glass, fall down manholes, think the gun is not loaded; disaster everywhere besets their ill-starred path. In a complementary way, Culbertson could be described as publicity-prone. Even when he did not try, he left a trail of publicity behind him like a comet's tail. As instance, the Beasley match. When Culbertson came to England it was ostensibly to win the Championship, but in reality to introduce his slam convention to the British public. While not actuated exclusively by motives of philanthropy, at the same time he felt he was conferring a boon on mankind, and that Bridge players from Leeds to London would rise up and call him blessed.

They rose up all right, but it was to do battle with each other, a civil war that has been waged with varying intensity ever since.

As ever, Buller was in the van. In 1931 he had written a book on his famous match with the Americans in which he makes it perfectly clear that a resounding victory was won by British Bridge. The actual result was incidental and due exclusively to "the bad play, bad bridge, and bad teamwork of my own team." To this comprehensive condemnation he generously makes one exception. "I was placed on performance easily top of all eight players." Regarding British Bridge he boomed ungrammatically, "None have ever beaten an experienced team playing whole-hog British Bridge, (which is) the Buller system, up to now not known as such, due to my modesty."

He now regarded his fellow officer as a renegade who, by adopting the traitorous Approach-Forcing methods, had gone over to the enemy. Had Buller known it he was to do worse: he was in the process of preparing his own system which would embody these very principles. However, that was in the future. For the present Buller was content to attribute the English defeat to their acceptance of an alien philosophy, and serve them right too! He anathematized with particular obloquy the 4-5 No Trump and cognate foreign conventions: "I am the originator and consistent advocate of the common-sense system. I am now generally accepted as having been right all the time." (Incidentally, his team was soon to be annihilated by one playing the Culbertson system.) "The time has now come finally to decide between direct and approach-forcing, myself and Culbertson. In this matter of principle no compromise is possible." Fighting words indeed, and worthy of the best traditions of the Army Service Corps in which he had soldiered.

The amazing thing is that a great number of people took this gallimaufry of nonsense quite seriously. By some curious process of doublethink Buller succeeded in persuading a considerable section of the public that Beasley's defeat was a victory for common sense, or British Bridge. The results were highly diverting. A pleasant feature of subscribing to the Buller credo lay in the fact that one did not have to learn anything about the principles of the game in order to play it with an air of authority. "Common Sense, Partner?" "Yes, of course," became a very usual, if expensive, piece of dialogue throughout the land. Unfortunately, if the opponents played to a system, it was generally the prelude to paying the stakes.

All this hoohah was unexpected by Culbertson who, paradoxically, had put himself forward as the apostle of natural, as opposed to artificial, bidding. He reconciled his own conventions with this conception as growing naturally out of the inherent character of the game. They invited partner "to draw beautiful and poetic references from the bidding," some were designed to "guide the partnership galleon past the hidden rocks of distribution." Buller described them less poetically as being "equivalent to blowing one's nose, scratching one's head, or other prearranged signal." A first-class row blew up and spread to wherever Bridge was played in England, which was by now almost everywhere. The antis equated some of the conventions, indeed a number condemned them all, as being no better than cheating. The pros regarded their antagonists as chauvinistic antediluvians, and said so. The newspapers took hands in the game, and eventually the Portland Club, in an olympian judgment, not only denounced the 4-5 No Trump as being unethical, but barred all artificial conventions of every description from defiling its vestal card rooms.

This had precisely the effect one would have anticipated. Such players as had ignored the controversy now felt there must be some considerable advantage in playing a convention which called down such condign proscription, and the Culbertson system flourished, supplying to its inventor an unexpected, unearned increment.

In the meantime, as yet unaware of the exciting developments which the Championship had touched off, Culbertson returned to America in the warm glow induced by something attempted, something done. But while most men would have considered they had earned a night's repose, he merely allowed himself and Jo a brief fortnight in Havana.

Culbertson returned from Havana to find himself in an unaccustomed role. Hitherto, of necessity, he had always been the challenger, now he discovered what it felt like to be the challenged. It was not at all a comfortable situation.

First there was the little matter of Albert Edye Manning-Foster, editor of the *Bridge Magazine* and undisputed leader of the British Bridge Establishment, whom Culbertson had outraged gratuitously and unforgivably. This sometime ally, now deadly foe, was largely responsible for the formation of the European Bridge League which held its championship in Grosvenor House in London the previous May. Anything less like a Culbertson promotion than this genteel affair it would be difficult to imagine, and it is equally difficult to fathom the motives which induced Manning-Foster to invite Mr. Culbertson as an observer. The fact remains that in an unguarded moment he did, with the unfortunate result that the observer, with an eye on his own forthcoming joust in Selfridges, gave an interview to the national press in which his comments on the play and arrangements were so pungent as to provoke a startled yelp of pain from his outraged host. The contrast of the triumphant Beasley match added injury to insult. The strains of a regular hymn of hate wafted across the Atlantic. Nor was this mere pique to be lightly disregarded because Foster had allied himself with the American Bridge League to form a world association from which Culbertson was excluded. This alone was a serious threat which called for resourceful counter-measures.

Nor was this all. The road to monopoly is indeed a rocky one beset with obstacles. He found also that in the War of the Systems, which seemed to have been finally won, yet two more notable battles must be fought before "Contract Bridge" and "Culbertson" became interchangeable terms.

While in no way neglecting these other problems, Culbertson found that his most formidable and immediate tasks lay in the jungle tracks of business. Nor was the Autumn of 1933 a very propitious moment in world economic history for such activities.

The America of the first year of Roosevelt hardly bears thinking about. The most popular song was "Buddy, can you spare a dime?" Very few could. The slogan of the National Recovery Act "We do our part" did not mean very much to twelve million unemployed who had enough to do trying to keep themselves warm. Big Business saw the President, with his brain trust and threat to pack the Supreme Court, as a red anarchist out to ruin the lot of them. No bright euphemist had dreamt up the soothing expression "recession"; this was the Big Depression and it did not occur to anyone to call it anything else.

It was typical of Culbertson that, not satisfied with shoring-up his already lucrative enterprises and waiting for better times, he decided then and there to expand them. In the teeth of the advice of such tycoons as Schwab, president of United States

Steel, and to the consternation of his own associates, he proceeded imperturbably to mortgage every last cent of his present and future on no other security than a colossal self-confidence.

First, he took out lavish endowment policies for Jo and their children so that in the knowledge that at least they were provided for, he could become happily bankrupt or spectacularly rich. In the single-minded pursuit of the latter objective he extended his ramifications into every conceivable industry which could remotely promote the prosperity of Contract Bridge. This he did either through his own companies, or in association with older corporations already established in other fields or countries which he wished to penetrate. Thus it was that by the outbreak of the war he could say for example, that his syndicated column circulated in fifty-eight countries in newspapers with a two hundred million readership. This did not take into account the very substantial achievements of Jo who monopolized, among others, the huge Hearst chain in succession to the defeated Official System.

Culbertson was also the first to appreciate that apart from playing cards, bridge players had other requirements, with the result that bridge tables, chairs, markers, tournament accessories and indeed all bridge equipment of any kind, brought an ever increasing stream of grist to his mill. Here, however, he was at first on unfamiliar territory, and his brash incursion into the playing card industry brought him almost to insolvency, and his manager, Al Morehead, and the terrified Jo, almost to an early grave. This was what he called his Kem Card Venture, although venture is a mild expression for a deal which in effrontery and bluff was in the best tradition of his spiritual ancestor, Phineas T. Barnum.

SCHWAB TROPHY
London 1933
BEASLEY v CULBERTSON

HAND 63

DEALER NORTH.

BOTH VULNERABLE.

NORTH
- ♠ K 8 7 3
- ♥ 7 4 3
- ♦ 7 5
- ♣ K J 4 2

WEST
Culbertson
Morris
- ♠ A 6 5 4 2
- ♥ K 10
- ♦ K 10
- ♣ A 10 6 3

EAST
Lightner
Tabbush
- ♠ 9
- ♥ A Q 8 6 5
- ♦ Q J 6 4 3 2
- ♣ 9

SOUTH
- ♠ Q J 10
- ♥ J 9 2
- ♦ A 9 8
- ♣ Q 8 7 5

Both Rooms

North	East	South	West
No	No	No	1 ♠
No	2 ♥	All Pass	

61

Result: 12 tricks made

Culbertson's comments on this, the outstanding fiasco of the match, is also an unwitting comment on the bidding philosophy, or lack of it, of the time:

An interesting hand. In both rooms a small Slam is made, and not even a game is bid. West vulnerable, has no re-bid and East is afraid to force, even though he passed, for fear of finding partner with Spades and Clubs, in which case it will probably end in disaster.

As can be seen, 6♥ or 6♦ is stiff, the latter being much the better contract. Diamonds, of course, were not even mentioned in either room.

Beasley does not even include it in his book on the match, nor does Phillips in his extracts. Of course, such catastrophes were common form in those carefree days.

BEASLEY V CULBERTSON
Selfridges, London, 1933

EAST DEALS.

N.S. VULNERABLE.

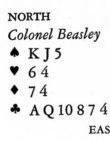

NORTH
Colonel Beasley
- ♠ K J 5
- ♥ 6 4
- ♦ 7 4
- ♣ A Q 10 8 7 4

WEST
Culbertson
- ♠ A Q 10 9 7 3
- ♥ Q J 9 2
- ♦ K 6 5
- ♣ —

EAST
Lightner
- ♠ 2
- ♥ K 10 8 7 5 3
- ♦ A Q J 2
- ♣ 5 2

SOUTH
Domville
- ♠ 8 6 4
- ♥ A
- ♦ 10 9 8 3
- ♣ K J 9 6 3

East	South	West	North
1 ♥	—	1 ♠	2 ♣
—	2 ♥	All Pass	

Lead Queen of Hearts.

Result: down 7 —1750 points.

This is the "Stark Tragedy for England" hand. The amount of the penalty may surprise modern eyes, but under the then system of scoring it increased in arithmetical progression per trick. It is true to say that if Sir Guy Domville's Two Heart bid, having passed, is somewhat outré, the Colonel's pass makes no sense at all. However, the hand fits beautifully into the insane pattern of the match.

BEASLEY V CULBERTSON
Selfridges, London, 1933

SOUTH DEALS.
BOTH VULNERABLE.

NORTH
Beasley
- ♠ J 4
- ♥ Q 8 7 4
- ♦ A 4 3
- ♣ J 6 3 2

WEST
Culbertson
- ♠ 10 9 8 7 5 3 2
- ♥ A K J
- ♦ K
- ♣ Q 5

EAST
Lightner
- ♠ A Q 6
- ♥ 6 5
- ♦ Q J 7 2
- ♣ K 10 8 7

SOUTH
Domville
- ♠ K
- ♥ 10 9 4 2
- ♦ 10 9 8 6 5
- ♣ A 9 4

South	West	North	East
—	—	—	1 ♦
—	1 ♠	All pass	

Result: E.W. make 11 tricks.

It passeth human understanding that even in 1933 a little old lady, much less the world's leading expert, could pass the West hand, and then, having been given another chance, not jump into Game.

Mr. Culbertson held the West hand, and Teddy Lightner the East, and the Maestro had the gall to comment in the Official History of the Match, "Having started the ball, Teddy might just as well have kept it rolling." How he expected his unfortunate partner to multiply his twelve miserable points he does not tell posterity. Posterity does know, however, that Lightner throughout was by far the best player who took part in the contest.

In the other room, the Englishmen, Morris and Tabbush, sailed into game, via One Spade, Three Spades, Four Spades, and made eleven tricks.

5

Mopping Up

Although the Kem Card nightmare was not to begin until 1935, it is difficult to credit that in the meantime Culbertson ever slept, for there was still a great deal to trouble his slumbers.

First of all, the American and European Leagues, having associated in an international organization, had declared war, largely through his provocation. He was preparing also his *Red Book on Play,* in addition to the *Gold Book,* unassumingly described by the author as *the* definitive work on the game. There was also daily concern with his business enterprises, newspaper columns, and *Bridge World.* As if all this were not enough, at the very moment of his international triumph he had to cope with two affronts to his dignity in the shapes respectively of the Four Aces, and Sims, systems.

Now if there is one thing quite clear about the otherwise precarious position he occupied at the end of 1933 it was that his system was not in danger, and no one was better aware of this than Mr. Culbertson himself. From that point of view, therefore, it was unnecessary to take on either the Four Aces, or P. Hal Sims. He decided, however, that when he had dealt with them in his own inimitable way the public, with its unerring flair for drawing the wrong conclusions, would regard the outcome as not merely vindicating his system, but as establishing the soundness of his other Bridge activities. In this he was not mistaken.

At this distance it would be profitless to expatiate on the differences between the two systems which were more fanciful than real. The strength of Four Aces lay in the prowess of its bashful inventors and exponents who supplied its title, Messrs. Gottlieb, Schenken, Burnstine, and the ubiquitous Ossie Jacoby. This prowess was such that while Culbertson was determined to deflate them he was taking no chances of being beaten by them, a fate which nearly befell him in England in the second Schwab match, against Lederer's team.

It is a measure of the adroit Ely's *sang froid* and ingenuity that, in spite of a calculatedly insulting challenge, he was able to downface his rivals without playing a card.

'Mike' Gottlieb was a wealthy real estate man. He was also a very fine Bridge player and was not at all gratified when Culbertson advised him to stick to property deals. As a token of his friendly concern Culbertson felt impelled to warn him also that if a match took place it would destroy the Aces. Instead he would bet him that the Four Aces book would not sell 10,000 copies in the ensuing year, rather less than the *Blue Book* sometimes sold in a week.

Nettled, in accordance with a formula Ely had perfected, Gottlieb bet $1,500, and in due course not only paid up but publicly and magnanimously announced: "Contract Bridge is now standardized on the principles set out in the Culbertson System." To such an extent was this pronouncement true that it received the accolade of judicial authority. When Culbertson brought an action to restrain a defendant from using the expression "Culbertson System" in his publicity, the court held that the phrase was public property and refused to intervene.

Needless to say, the resourceful Maestro turned this legal defeat to good account. He supplemented the learned judge's observations, which had clearly not gone far enough, in his own luxuriant prose:

"By the Spring of 1934 I had completed a world-wide organization that far surpassed the combined publicity set-ups of a great motion-picture star, a radio idol, a famous writer, a captain of industry, and a champion prize-fighter."

It will be noticed that Ely, clearly a religious man, makes no extravagant comparisons with the Deity.

This laudable reserve however, did not extend to Mr. P. Hal Sims or his system, or his effrontery which amounted to *lèse majesté*. Not the least of his crimes was his treasonable alliance with the British and European Bridge Leagues, which bodies treated Culbertson and all his works with anathema and contempt. Indeed, the previous October, Sims made common cause with Manning-Foster, editor of the *Bridge Magazine* and Ely's deadly foe, by making him a life member of the American Bridge League. Nor was he content with this calculated indignity; in the very month of the Four Aces contretemps he published a letter in Foster's magazine in which he deplored the references to that gentleman in "a publication called the *Bridge World.*"

This, although grossly insulting, was meat and drink to the *Bridge World's* editor who replied with unwonted restraint: "There is a large enough body of Sims' adherents to put the two systems to the test and allow the public to compare results." Although the public might well have asked, "Where have we heard all this before?" they lapped it up.

It is difficult to conceive of two more antipathetic characters than these antagonists. In contrast to the slim, urbane, if sardonic Culbertson, Sims, who stood six foot four and weighed 275 pounds, had about as much urbanity in his makeup as a bull elephant. When in a national championship that summer he slapped (who else?) Oswald Jacoby on the face "for boisterously laughing at him," he hit the headlines to such effect that the echoes are to be heard to this day.

But Hal Sims also happened to be one of the world's best bridge players. He was probably the outstanding player of the famous Four Horsemen team, who had won every important tournament for three years, and whose first defeat, in the autumn of 1931, caused a greater sensation than any of their victories. He was also one of the experts of Official System fame, and undaunted by its defeat in the Battle of the Century, had since evolved his own.

The Sims system had many good features, several of which were purloined without acknowledgement by the eclectic Ely. It is rather unfair that it is best remembered now for its famous Sims Three Bid. It has been said that this brainchild of its ingenious inventor was the most perfect bid in bridge, being subject only to the slight handicap that the requirements for it occurred, on an average, about once every six months.

The stage was set in every respect, for Sims, like Culbertson, had also a bridge-playing wife. She was petite, attractive, and as dynamic as her husband. It was inevitable that the match should be between Hal and Dorothy against Ely and Jo over 150 rubbers, each side playing its own system.

Because of Culbertson's almost superhuman commitments, including a return visit to England, and because of the now conventional orgy of publicity, the game did not take place until the end of March and beginning of April 1935. It was worth waiting for, if only because of its background and the personalities of the contestants who cordially loathed each other. The interest as far as the United States was concerned was second only to the Lenz match, and the preparations almost as elaborate, as witness Culbertson himself who was so uniquely qualified in this department:

"The match is held in the playing room of Crockfords Club in New York. Two large rooms have been set aside for the match and have been decorated at great cost to provide the ultimate in comfort for the players, and yet to admit a few spectators. Around the room are placed platforms on which there are chairs for invited guests. The centre of the ring is guarded by heavy silk ropes strung between heavy chromium stanchions. The chairs and tables were built to order for the four players. Sims weighs 275 pounds and is six feet four inches tall.

"Above the table is a 'mike' of a radio station carrying to millions of listeners reports of the progress of the match, and every word spoken by the contestants, in bidding, in discussing the hands, or in the half-friendly, half-bitter badinage which is constantly being exchanged. Beside the table sit referees and hand recorders. In a second room dozens of newspaper reporters hand out their stories, and telegraph operators in the same room transmit theirs to thousands of newspapers at the rate of 150,000 words per diem."

Sidney Horatio Lenz must have felt at home in these cozy surroundings, because he was there as guest of honor at the invitation of his erstwhile rival; or perhaps as a historian it reminded him of the meeting of Henry of England and Francis of France on the Field of the Cloth of Gold. Probably it did not, for no such civilities as were exchanged between those medieval monarchs graced the lush pastures of Crockfords—very much the contrary.

Despite all the flummery and publicity buildup this, the last major joust of Culbertson's career, was also the last important. It had one *raison d'etre,* pure unadulterated bitchiness, and one object, the satisfaction of personal spleen. In this regard it was the most notable of Ely's successes inasmuch as after it, and to the day he died, Sims was never known to write or say a word about his antagonist without manifesting an acute nausea. This disposition was hardly moderated by the memory of the unmerciful beating he took in a match he so badly wanted to win.

Of the match itself, apart from the now traditional codology, there is very little to be said. As usual, the Culbertsons trailed for a few early rubbers, and for two days the flag again flew at half-mast over Crockfords. Thereafter it waved triumphantly in a balmy breeze until the final tally of 16,130 points was totted up.

The *Bridge World* supplied an additional dose of gall in

pointing out that, although getting the better of the cards, Sims won only 69 of the 150 rubbers played.

By April 1935 Culbertson had in twelve months disposed of his two outstanding rivals in the United States. It is worthy of mention that in the meantime, October to be precise, he had retained the Schwab Trophy by defeating the strongest team he had ever met, the British champions headed by Richard Lederer, playing the Lederer Club, a system which until that match had been enjoying a certain vogue.

All in all it was just as well for Culbertson's remarkable equanimity that he had disposed of these distractions, because it was at this juncture that two middle-European gentlemen called at his office on Lexington Avenue. They presented him diffidently with a proposition that brought him enthusiastically to the verge of bankruptcy, and eventually made him a fortune.

It was one of Culbertson's more endearing qualities that he was prepared to see anyone at any time. As we know, travellers in toilet paper had an equal entrée to the presence as did distillers of whiskey. Were it not for this gregarious trait it is doubtful if on a spring morning in 1935 either Siegfried Klausner or Robert Caro would have got beyond the receptionist. Certainly their appearance was not calculated to cause a secretary to take out her lipstick, or a businessman his check book. They looked exactly what they were, two forlorn and rather shabby nonconformists to a New Order that was in the process of ravishing their continent.

Culbertson's first reaction was to pity them, but the naiveté of their opening gambit made him laugh.

"Mr. Culbertson, we have come to you as a last resort."

"I take it you have tried everywhere else, then?"

"Everywhere, Mr. Culbertson, without success."

Controlling himself, he asked what they wanted him to do for them.

"Merely to look at these, sir."

With a slight flourish "these" were laid on his desk, and turned out to be a rather crudely produced pack of playing cards.

Culbertson was convinced that he was on the receiving end of another of those crackpot visitations to which he was accident-prone. However, something in their manner made him listen, and as they went on they began to make more sense.

It appeared that they had invented a new type of playing card which was so superior to the conventional as to be revolutionary. They knew that Culbertson had nothing to do with the manufacture of cards, but having heard that he was receptive to new ideas they had finally come to him. They had no money and no plant, hence the unfinished appearance of their cards. But the cards had other qualities which were unique, they were washable, noninflammable, germ-proof, and would outlast fifty packs of the best quality cards in existence. They calculated they could be produced for three dollars as against twenty cents for an ordinary pack. Even at that, and apart from their other advantages, the cards represented a good bargain. They owed their virtues to the inventors' discovery and perfection of a process whereby plastic-acetate could be adapted to the needs of playing cards.

Now, this was exactly the sort of thing which was calculated to capture the imagination of the ebullient Ely. He was interested, and when he was interested he acted fast. With the same sort of insouciance which had made him a publisher, he became a card manufacturer, and with even less knowledge of what was involved. He gave the inventors a third interest, opened a bank account for $5,000 for them and went to work.

In short order the Western Playing Card Company Inc. was born, and Culbertson proceeded to enlist the aid of every firm that could possibly further the project. The Du Pont, Celanese, and Fiberloid companies all gave him the services of their technicians and the use of their laboratories. Other firms looked after the lacquer, varnish, and inks, while he himself designed a permanent plastic box to house his product, which he christened KEM Cards for the esoteric reason that a chemical process was involved in their manufacture.

For the merchandising of Kem he called on his thousands

of teachers, bridge clubs in every State, nearly all the leading stores, as well as employing every extravaganza of publicity as occurred to his fertile invention.

As a direct result of the activities, and his remarkable energy and foresight, twelve months after the momentous visit of Messrs. Klausner and Caro, his accountants were in a position to inform him that Kem had cost him over two hundred thousand dollars.

Ely Culbertson, author and journalist, editor and publisher, industrialist and now manufacturer, was made aware by this unwelcome piece of information that he was in the unique position of having a huge income, yet unable to pay his hotel bills. His *Red Book on Play* was selling by the hundred thousand, and his *Gold Book,* just published, was to sell over two million copies all over the world. All his other enterprises were expanding and, with the exception of Kem, flourishing. He had outstripped or beaten all other rivals in America and England. His position should have been impregnable.

The paradox was inherent in his highly individual system of economics, founded on the fundamental law of All or Nothing. From this unorthodox and hazardous philosophy he never apostatized. As has been seen, in each of his ventures from the foundation of the *Bridge World,* such as the Buller and Lenz matches and the publication of the *Blue Book,* he balanced his entire future on a razor's edge, and he was in the process of completing the pattern with the Kem Cards gamble.

There was, however, a radical and far-reaching difference between this and his previous adventures, which has never before been realized—in all probability the sanguine Ely did not appreciate it himself: this time he was placing the entire future of Contract Bridge itself in the balance!

The reasons for this extraordinary situation were the monolithic nature of the organization he had created and his elimination of effective competition. In 1936, he was first referred to as The Emperor of Bridge, and the title was not as hyperbolic as it sounds. At the same time, while his empire was worldwide, to consolidate it it was necessary not merely to plough back every cent of income, but to borrow right, left and center. In Bradstreet his credit rating was "Slow"—a distinct euphemism. The result was that if Culbertson failed at this juncture, the whole monopolistic edifice he had built would have come down with him, appropriately, like a house of cards. It is interesting to speculate whether or not in the result the game would have been reduced to a passing fad like Canasta or Gin Rummy, as indeed it was when he took over in 1929. It is certain that a vacuum would have been created and Contract Bridge could not have developed into the global institution we know today.

In these circumstances one would have though he would have jumped at anything to relieve him of the incubus of Kem. Far from that, he refused every offer until Jo and Morehead were reduced to nervous prostration.

The first offer came in April 1936, when he was visited by three gentlemen who produced a checkbook and made him a firm offer of $300,000 in cash for the outright property in Kem. Jo, who was present, nearly died when her husband informed the tycoons that if they started at half a million cash, the other details could be ironed out later. That concluded the interview, and when Jo was tactless enough to refer to some outstanding and pressing accounts, she was informed: "Never mind, darling, they'll be back."

Sure enough, they did come back—in October, six months later, this time with a lawyer and a contract. The offer was now half a million, take it or leave it. Both Jo and Morehead were stunned to hear Culbertson say, "I'm sorry, gentlemen, the price is six hundred thousand, and 5 percent on the U.S. rights."

When the four angry visitors had stamped out of the office, Jo was speechless and Morehead pungently expressed his opinion that his principal was in urgent need of the best psychiatrist in the country, or better still, a team of psychiatrists.

Culbertson was, in fact, frightened at himself, although he did not show it. "They want Kem very badly, just wait."

They did wait—for three agonizing months.

In January 1937 back marched the gentlemen again. This time Culbertson was ready for them with a contract drawn up by his own lawyer. Six hundred thousand cash, 5 percent of the U.S. gross for fifteen years, and world rights reserved for himself.

The gentlemen exploded. And when the imperturbable Ely said that those were his final terms, one of them barked that it was impossible to do business on such a ridiculous basis, slammed the contract on the desk and the door behind his departing colleagues.

The faithful and suffering Morehead, who probably knew Culbertson's affairs better than he knew them himself, was a broken man.

"Now you have really done it, this time they won't be back."

"Did you notice, Al, he threw the contract on the desk? He didn't throw it at me. They'll be back all right."

For three of the longest days of their lives they waited. Culbertson had turned his office into a cocktail bar, and kept his lawyer continuously on tap. He said later that once they entered the office they would be treated as if the whole transaction were concluded. Miraculously, that is how it worked out. On the third day the Kem contract was signed, sealed and delivered. Six hundred thousand cash, and the other rights as demanded. Cocktails were duly served all round.

Three months later Ely saw his accountants again. The interview was in remarkable contrast to its counterpart the previous year. All his debts were paid and the millions were pouring in: it was the zenith of his career.

The Emperor of Bridge was established at last on a solid throne.

CULBERTSON V SIMS
CHALLENGE MATCH
Crockford's Club, New York, 1935

WEST DEALS.

BOTH VULNERABLE.

NORTH
Jo Culbertson
- ♠ Q J 7
- ♥ J 5 4 3
- ♦ 9
- ♣ A K 10 5 2

WEST
P. Hal Sims
- ♠ A
- ♥ 10 8 6 2
- ♦ K Q J 8 6
- ♣ J 9 7

EAST
Dorothy Sims
- ♠ 10 9 6 4 3
- ♥ 7
- ♦ 7 5 3 2
- ♣ Q 6 3

SOUTH
Ely Culbertson
- ♠ K 8 5 2
- ♥ A K Q 9
- ♦ A 10 4
- ♣ 8 4

West	North	East	South
—	—	—	1 ♥
—	2 ♣	—	2 ♠
—	5 ♥	All Pass	

Result: 11 tricks made.

This was the most hilarious and publicized hand in the Sims-Culbertson ballyhoo epic. It occurred shortly after Ely had allotted spaces for the players' feet, and the atmosphere was somewhat charged.

The play was as peculiar as the bidding. Sims led the King of Diamonds, won by the Ace. Then came the Ace and King of Hearts, and a spade, won by the Ace. Sims now led a diamond ruffed in Dummy, and Ely went into a prolonged trance.

"What are you thinking about?" enquired Dorothy.

"Cogito ergo sum," replied the erudite Ely.

"Speak English, professor," Mr. Sims observed.

"I am considering," said Culbertson, "whether I am going down one or two."

He then led the Knave of Spades which Sims ruffed, and returned another Diamond trumped in Dummy. Culbertson was now able to set up the Club suit with a ruff, draw the last trump, and return to the established Clubs via the Queen of Spades.

Sims created blue hell, because he said he had been misled by Culbertson's remark about going down, but the referee was not impressed.

If Sims had discarded a Club on the Knave of Spades the contract was sunk, but equally, if Ely had cashed the Ace and Knave of Hearts at the second and third tricks, there was no defense.

He never spoke more truthfully than when he said:

"I play men, not cards."

6

The Tight Little Isle

It entails a considerable effort of reorientation, no less
mental than geographical, to transfer our attention to the
English scene, where events had taken a very different course
from the febrile goings-on across the ocean. Admittedly, in
England also there had arisen a dominating personality, if the
epithet is permissible, but apart from that sole phenomenon
there was no other parallel. Whereas, the impact made by the
effervescent Ely was as dynamic as an atom bomb, that of
Manning-Foster was more reminiscent of the resounding plop
of a suet pudding on a concrete floor.

Albert Edye Manning-Foster, the hyphen was a later recognition of services rendered, had successfully pursued at Public
School and University that conventionally undistinguished
academic career which was calculated to insulate a gentleman
against such disturbing processes of thought as might have
otherwise assailed him. On leaving Oxford he was admitted to
the degree of Barrister-at-Law by the Benchers of the Inner
Temple. One feels that that honorable society must have
viewed his later career with a sense of disappointment that
he did not continue, or indeed begin, his practice in the courts.
He would probably have brought great credit on his Inn by his
elevation to the bench, for he had all those qualities of the ideal

78

judge which were attributed to the late Baron Huddleston. He
was slow, he was courteous, he was wrong.

Mr. Foster while no doubt aware of the preferment these
qualities would in time confer upon a practitioner at the
Chancery Bar, decided to devote them to a more immediate
advantage. Accordingly, he had himself elected to some of the
leading London clubs, the card rooms of which he attended
with an assiduity and dedication which eventually brought him
the ultimate guerdon of a seat on the Card Committee of the
Portland. The law courts never saw him more.

One other trait which conditioned Mr. Foster's attitude to
life, Bridge, and everything else, was the most highly developed
sense of snobbery since Beau Nash. A couple of extracts from
the *Bridge Magazine* are typical.

In the issue for June 1931 its readers were regaled with this
exciting news scoop apropos a Bridge tournament at London-
derry House: "Among the players were Lady Helena Acland-
Hood, Lady Crosfield, Lady Buckingham, Mary, Lady Clancarty,
Sybil, Lady Brassey, Lady Lloyd." and ten other titled *mesdames,*
the blue-blooded attendance being further distinguished by the
presence of Mr. Manning-Foster and Lady Oxford and Asquith.

In May of the previous year, on the fourth anniversary of
Bridge Magazine, in the list of birthday messages pride of place
was given in bold lettering to those, in descending order, from
the Marchioness of Winchester, Viscount Doneraile, and Sir
Robert Leicester Harmsworth, Bart. "Colonel Hopton of Led-
bury informed us how much it was appreciated in the country-
house." One can almost hear the editor purring.

This, then, was the man who under the aegis of John Waddington Ltd. the card manufacturers, started the *Auction Bridge
Magazine* in May 1926.

It was typical of its editor that it was published under that
title in the very year that Contract was introduced to, and was
soon to sweep, the United States. As late as September 1929, the
month in which the Work-Whitehead Auction magazine died of
inanition, Mr. Foster delivered himself of this gem in his

editorial: "It is now evident that there is going to be no such landslide in favour of Contract as many people anticipate. . . . Those who play Bridge more as a relaxation and love its subtler qualities will cling to Auction and they are probably a majority."

The most appropriate comment on this inspired prophecy came from the prophet himself three months later when he informed his readers that as from the following month the title would be altered to *Bridge Magazine* on the grounds: "Contract has, we are assured, come to stay, and while it has not yet superseded Auction, it is probable that in course of time it will become the paramount game."

What exactly he meant by "course of time" is characteristically obscure; it is sufficient to observe that nine months later the Buller-Culbertson match was played and the *Blue Book* published, with results of which we are aware.

It is hardly surprising that such an idiosyncratic editor should attract into his literary orbit contributors so much in accord with his propensities as to differ from each other only in degree of fatuity. As a recruiting ground he not unnaturally looked to the Army, who, as ever, responded to the call. The result was a roster of warrior journalists, which one would be forgiven for assuming had been compiled in the War Office from its files of literate officers of field rank. It is fair to record that while Manning - Foster leaned heavily on the soldiery he did not neglect the civil arm as represented by the nobility and gentry. If the peasantry was kept in its proper place he clearly had the cultured condescension of a gentleman to the polite arts, notably poetry of a nostalgic genre, redolent of lavender water and snowy cambric lace, as witness:

MUSETTE

When the autumn mists are rising from their
    parklands far from town,
Silver-haired my Lord and Lady to their
    'Parti' sit them down.

> But across the rose-lit table in the
>   log-fire's generous glow,
> Comes a vision: 'Boodle's crowded; just like
>   White's,—how long ago!
> Wonder what the youngster's up to; like his
>   Father, I'm afraid!
> Better just run up and see him. . . . Yes, my love,
>   the Cards are made.'

Under the stress of great emotion Albert Edye himself could rhapsodize with Grantland Rice:

> And when the last Great Scorer cometh
> To write against your name,
> He'll ask not if you won or lost
> But how you played the game.

This imaginative and manly admonishment was occasioned during his flaming row with the cynical Mr. Culbertson. It is surely unwarranted, as has been suggested, that this attitude was possibly aggravated by the sales of the *Blue Book* exceeding those of his own works in the ratio of roughly a thousand to one.

It would also be unjust, as well as unchivalrous, to pass from the poetry of the *Bridge Magazine* without paying tribute to Mrs. E. Sefi, the unsung poetess of Kensington, who did so much to lighten the cares of the prewar decade, or would have done if the fruits of her lyric genius had been tasted by a wider public.

It can be said that when the Scottish poet Mordaunt delivered himself of,

> One crowded hour of glorious life,
> Is worth an age without a name

once, and once only, had he stood on Mount Olympus; but he had his crowded hour. Similarly, when the reverend winner of the Newdigate soared to the heights of,

> A rose-red city, half as old as time

he fell back exhausted on the laurels of a rural deanery, all passion spent.

It must also be conceded that such versifiers as Longfellow, Ella Wheeler Wilcox, even the late great laureate Alfred Austin sometimes so deviated from their appalling standards as to write a couplet, or perhaps a verse, not actively emetic. Among this galaxy Mrs. E. Sefi is remarkable, for if ever she wrote a non-bad line, the most rigorous research has failed to bring it to light.

As an anthology would be needed to show her talents in their luxuriance, one example must, perforce, suffice:

HONOURS

She played a lone' hand' and the whole world
    was thrilled.
She 'bridged' all those miles, and her
    'contract' fulfilled.
She had courage and skill and the coolness
    enough
To 'score' and to 'win' in despite of the
    'rough'.
She deserves all her luck and her rise into fame.
For being a 'Trump' and entirely 'game'.
She's a 'Card', and her value we really can't place.
She's a 'Queen' right enough, but she's also an 'Ace'!

So compulsive is the poetic muse that for upwards of ten years Mrs. Sefi was an incessant and unrelenting contributor to the magazine; so much so that only the outbreak of a world war succeeded in damming the flow of her inspiration when publication was suspended in September 1939.

No less remarkable in the sterner tutorial field were the contributions of the military and civilian pundits. Each propounded his own peculiar system, and for once the adjective can be used in its pedantic and popular senses, for none of these systems had anything in common other than a variable, if inveterate, norm of lunacy.

An examination of the theories expounded by these experts would be more appropriate to a psychiatric textbook but even the layman should appreciate passing reference to a few of the more outlandish theses.

Possibly the most attractive was that advocated by Lord Tollemache who in a lengthy but entertaining series displayed the beauties of his Chronological Order System.

In this departure from humdrum precedent His Lordship advocated a novel method of card evalution for which he could claim an exclusive copyright, which is never likely to be infringed. In this unusual system Ace was valued at £1; the King, ten shillings; Queen, five shillings; Knave, half a crown; the ten, one and sixpence, and each other card at a shilling. This had the consolatory merit of allowing the holder of even a Yarborough the feeling of frugal comfort induced by the possession of thirteen bob. Unfortunately, the series petered out before its aristocratic author translated its complexities into foreign currency, which during the 1930s would have represented an economic *tour de force* worthy of Dr. Hjalmar Schacht.

Another pioneer in the field of Bridge insanity was Lieutenant-Colonel A. D. Jameson, D.S.O., M.C., whose system merits at least a mention in dispatches, if only because the author's bravery on the field of battle was no less conspicuously displayed at the card-table if he practiced there the precepts he enjoined upon his readers. Among the more singular of these was a recommendation that a player should open the bidding on two bare Aces and nothing else of value in the hand. As this exiguous holding represents rather less than one-fifth of the honor strength available in any given deal it can be said to be the Bridge equivalent of playing Russian roulette with five of the revolver's chambers loaded. There was in addition the not inconsiderable risk that a similar weapon was concealed on one's partner's person.

Lest it be thought that the methods advocated by Lord Tollemache and Colonel Jameson are maliciously selected, let it be said at once that they formed only part of an exquisitely symmetrical pattern of error with which Manning - Foster adorned his magazine. This included articles almost every month by Major F. P. Barton who was unable to arrive at the right conclusion, even by mistake.

There were also the Pachabo System, the 7-13 System of P. G. Silley, M.A. (not a *nom de plume*), and the aptly named Recoil System, as well as a host of others which if they sank almost on launching, did not do so without trace for by and large they all helped to bedevil Bridge in England for years. One would be pardoned for concluding that all this was part of an elaborate leg-pull on the public, such as Samuel Butler's *The Fair Haven,* were it not that Manning-Foster himself published his own definitive work on the game entitled *English Contract Bridge,* a compendium of heresy so flagrant as to prompt the conviction that were there a Bridge *auto-da-fé* its author would infallibly have been burned at the stake. This opinion is not borne out by the full page advertisements for this opus which quoted eulogistic excerpts from the press reviews. These prominently included one from *The Observer* which said "No better book has been written . . ." and another from *The Field,* "A valuable work which every player ought to possess." No doubt only his natural modesty restrained the author from informing readers of the *Bridge Magazine* that he was Cards Editor of both these influential publications.

The motto of the magazine was Play Better Bridge, and the avowed object of these systems and theories was to educate the average player and improve the expert. At the same time the services of a Mr. H. L. Thornely were enlisted to write an almost interminable series called Bridge Dialogues for Beginners.

The scene, we are told, is laid in "any smoke room," and the *dramatis personae* are the beginner and the expert, who are respectively and revoltingly christened Novis and Coatch. The dialogue has its own hypnotic fascination, but even greater interest lies in the psychopathy of the two personalities.

Novis is perhaps the more interesting study inasmuch as he displays all the characteristics of a low grade mental defective suffering from advanced melancholia. This condition manifests itself in occasional outbursts of rebellion ("Jove, but dash it all Coatch, I am in a worse muddle than when I started"), while ordinarily his condition is one of an abject humility compared with which the attitude of the late little Alice Ben Bolt would seem more like the vehemence of an unpaid madam.

Coatch, on the other hand, is a megalomaniac of almost Hitlerian proportions, to which he allies a complacency which expresses itself in an insufferable mock-modesty calculated to make the strongest wince. For instance:

NOVIS: How easy it is Coatch to mess things up. "The little slip and what worlds away"—to paraphrase Browning.

COATCH: Yet another bloomer, Novis?

NOVIS: (having informed him what occurred) Now Coatch, how would you have played the hand?

COATCH: Fairly obvious, Novis. If the adverse trumps are equally divided and—

NOVIS: As it happens they were.

COATCH: Very well then. Ruff the third round of spades with the nine of hearts——

NOVIS: Dash it, Coatch, do make a slip for once in a way.

COATCH: Oh, I can do that all right, if you'll produce something really difficult.

This Socratic dialogue went on for three more pages, and was obviously so attuned to the taste of the readers that the series ran for over two years. All the same it is difficult to believe that any beginner who followed the fortunes of Novis and Coatch for even two months could ever afterwards look a court card between the eyes without throwing up.

Finally, and painful though it be, duty compels reference to the features which were intended to be funny. The particular brand of humor favored by the editor was of a type seldom found outside the pages of the prewar *Punch,* as if Winnie-the-Pooh had mated with Billy Bunter and produced a monster of terrifying and hearty whimsy. In the supply of entertainment of this genre Manning-Foster was again well served by his contributors, foremost among whom were Captain Hugh Tuite, and a humorist of peculiar virulence called M. O. Sale.

Mr. Sale, who displayed a chauvinistic patriotism worthy of the great Buller himself, flung most of his squibs at American methods, which he considered inferior to the honest and downright approach of the bulldog breed. For example, apropos Culbertson's advocacy of the honor-trick count he commented with Wildean drollery, "Avoid *vulgar* fractions, Contract is a game for ladies and gents." And again, partner having made a bad bid, he suggests, "Throw him out on the pavement, where he will be able to rearrange his thoughts on a *concrete* basis." Believe it or not, he finished that particular effusion, "I am going back to my coal black mammy in Minnehaha." Ah well!

Anyone seeking relief from the gloom engendered by the humor of Mr. Sale in the coruscating wit of Captain Tuite was due for a severe traumatic shock. One reads Captain Tuite with that kind of fascinated horror which James Agate tells us overcame him on first reading Henry James's *Turn of the Screw.*

This happy warrior was invariably introduced as the author of *The Pottleton Bridge Club, Contract Bridge for Iris, Teaching Iris Auction Bridge* &. &. While one can only speculate upon the sinister implications of those ampersands, the titles of his other works express that cozy style so inimitably his own. Disdaining such unoriginal orientations at the card table as the geographical points N-S, E-W, or even the conservative A-B, Z-Y, he invested these letters with personalities and a nomenclature which Marie Corelli or Ethel M. Dell might well have envied. His card tables were accordingly populated by such improbable representatives of the upper crust as Lady Mastodon, Mr. Fairfield, a Senior Wrangler, Colonel Buzzard, The Vicar, and a coven of weird females such as Mrs. Pottleton herself,

Miss Fuselle, Miss Cardrop, and Mrs. Drone, who presumably arrived by broomstick.

Not content with this highly individual brand of *divertissement,* Captain Tuite sometimes displayed his versatility by trespassing on the territory of his colleague, M. O. Sale, and even outdid that acknowledged master in his own field. To show his mettle, perhaps it is permitted to cull two examples from an article headed with unbearable, if typical, coyness:

EXTRA SPECIAL ANSWERS

(One guinea per Reply: N.B.—cheques to be made payable to me, *not* to the Editor.)

TUT TUT (TOOTING)

'Contract does not imply "shrinking" from an original call. I echo your pseudonym.'

and

THREE ARTS (DEAL)

'You've lost your bet. Hoyle isn't a lubricant.'

It will be appreciated by now that Manning-Foster was prepared to publish literally anything. In the nature of things an occasional article that made sense crept in, almost invariably from the odd American writer. But these articles, submerged as they were in the surrounding gallimaufry, made no impact whatsoever. Confusion had made its masterpiece, and in a publication occupying a position in the British bridge playing world comparable to that of, say, *The Lancet* in the medical.

At the same time the historian should be grateful to Manning-Foster and his magazine, for it furnishes him with incontrovertible and unique evidence of the depths in which the bridge élite of England wallowed in the thirties; by inference he can also contemplate the abject condition of the card-playing serfs in those medieval days.

The effect of the magazine upon the advancement of the game is harder to assess. Certainly, as will be seen, there were some outstandingly good players in England, but very few compared with the misguided multitude. All in all, having regard to the progress of the game in other European countries and America, it can justifiably be said that its natural development was effectively retarded in Britain for the best part of twenty years, and the foot that pressed the hardest on the brake belonged to Albert Edye Manning-Foster.

Perhaps the most significant tribute that can be paid to his tutelage and influence is the fact that Britain had to wait until 1948 to win her first European championship.

7

The Love-Hate Life of Ely and Albert

Mention has been made of the harassment of Mr. Culbertson on his triumphal return to the States after his win over Colonel "Pops" Beasley in the historic match at Selfridges. It will be remembered that not the least of the cares which beset him was the formation of an international bridge organization from which he was excluded, and which constituted a challenge serious enough to threaten the entire fabric of his authority.

The story of this zany warfare would be worth recording for its intrinsic entertainment value even had nothing come of it. Oddly enough a great deal did come of it, and what started in a fit of spinsterish spite by Manning-Foster ended, when eventually peace was declared, in the formation of an international body, the successor of which today exercises sole and undisputed authority over competitive bridge the world over.

It is ironical that the fates should have chosen so unlikely an instrument as the egregious Albert Edye to effect such a consummation. It should be added that Ely himself contributed in no small measure to provoking hostilities by pricking him where it caused the greatest pain, in his *amour propre*. During the heat of the ensuing battles he once informed W. C. Fields

89

that he should amend his golden rule "Never give a sucker an even break" to "Never give a sucker a break at all."

In order to put the conflict in proper perspective it is necessary to go back to the Buller-Culbertson match of 1930.

When Culbertson engaged that ebullient warrior in the roped arena of Almacks in London, he not only laid the foundation of his fortunes, he also introduced duplicate bridge to a country where hitherto it had been almost unknown.

At the beginning of 1939 the number of bridge players in England was estimated at one and a half million, while those playing, or playing at, duplicate had increased from almost zero in 1930 to fifteen thousand. Today the respective figures, although approximate, are five million and 25,000. This estimate would appear to be borne out by the City Section of the *Sunday Times,* which, when announcing the merger in the Spring of 1963, of De la Rue and Waddington, expressed the playing-card business of these firms at £2,000,000 per annum. These figures, large as they appear, are minuscule compared with the United States where there are said to be thirty million players. The proportion who play duplicate is anybody's guess, but an entry of five or six thousand for a big tournament is commonplace. In Los Angeles in 1958, 6,154 tables were in play during the week in a tournament which, it is hardly necessary to add, was on television.

Although duplicate was unknown in England in 1930, it was otherwise in America. As far back as 1891 Cassius McBaine and J. L. Sebring perfected the tray in which the four hands of cards were placed in duplicate in Whist tournaments. The following year John T. Mitchell of Chicago devised a movement for eight to forty pairs which is still in use, and which provides two winning pairs, one for the North-South cards and one for the East-West.

In 1897, Edwin C. Howell of Boston produced a more elaborate movement for any number, whereby each pair played every other, and one winning pair only emerged from the tournament. These are basically the two movements from which the complicated structure of modern tournaments both for pairs and teams of four has grown up.

The popularity of duplicate Whist, and later Auction Bridge, was immediate, and when Contract swept the country the ground was well prepared for duplicate Contract tournaments which became the rage. This, in turn, led to a proliferation of warring associations, domestic fury, and fierce civil strife, an atmosphere in which Culbertson was happily, indeed enthusiastically, at home.

As early as 1927 Richard R. Richards, with a devotion to uniformity which his symmetrical name implies, founded and appointed himself first president of the American Bridge League. While his avowed object was to bring order and good government to the anarchical state of duplicate Bridge, what in fact he succeeded in doing was to create chaos out of confusion, for he had omitted to inform Mr. Ely Culbertson of his masterplan or to admit him to his counsels. This was an affront to majesty not lightly to be borne or forgotten—nor was it!

Later, when the preparations for the Buller match were under way, Ely appointed Manning-Foster a member of the English committee in charge of the arrangements. It never occurred to the artless Albert that this distinction was not unconnected with his editorship of the *Bridge Magazine,* rather did he attribute it to a proper recognition of his sterling worth by the American master.

Manning-Foster was happy. He was doubly delighted when the contest blasted Buller and his British Bridge, because that forthright gentleman and Mr. Foster did not laugh at each other's jokes. In fact, Colonel Walter Buller was in the habit of metaphorically picking up Mr. Foster in his teeth and worrying him rather as an angry bulldog would an annoying peke. Epithets such as bumblepuppy and nincompoop, as he was wont to apply to the editor of the *Bridge Magazine,* would have been visited with sternest reprimand if used in his regimental mess. From Manning-Foster they merely provoked an occasional bleat of dignified distress.

The first fruits of the short honeymoon of Albert and Ely, as the latter had astutely foreseen, was that the former became an immediate convert to the approach-forcing principles of Bridge, however imperfectly he understood them.

In the rarefied circles of the aristocracy which were the chosen habitat of Albert, the Culbertson system became the *dernier cri* for a time. In the magazine itself a profusion of advertisements of Bridge schools run by certificated Culbertson teachers appeared as if by magic.

The idyll achieved its apogee in 1931 when Mr. Foster as founder, first president, and sole member of the British Bridge League, appointed the London Culbertson Studio as the official school for its members, thereby provoking Buller, ever vigilant as Cato for the honor of his country, to near apoplexy. In the columns of Lord Beaverbrook's *Daily Express* Buller called down anathema upon the traitor who was pandering to the Americans and sabotaging British Bridge in the process. With sibylline prevision he foretold that Manning-Foster would rue his faithless alliance.

For once, perhaps for the only time in his life, the Colonel was right, and he had not long to wait.

In February 1932, immediately after the Battle of the Century with Lenz, there appeared the tiniest rift within the lute.

In an editorial stamped with that dignity but firmness one would expect, under the by-line "Mr. R. R. Richards," the editor protested against an unwarranted plagiarism perpetrated by that gentleman in the November issue of the *Bridge World*. This, he alleged, appeared in an article entitled How to be a Good Player and was taken word for word from his own *Auction Bridge for All,* without acknowledgement. As this was probably the only time in history that anything Manning-Foster ever wrote was quoted with approval except in his own magazine, one would have thought he could have let the hare sit.

He wrote to Richards and the *Bridge World.* The former did not reply at all, but from the Culbertson National Studio on December 3 came, "On Mr. Culbertson's behalf I want to personally apologize for this mistake and trust you will believe that any infringement on author's rights was quite unintentional.' Manning-Foster felt this was inadequate, and that the disclaimer should appear under Culbertson's name in the *Bridge World*. Having had a sideswipe at the ethics of the taciturn Mr. Richards he concluded his editorial: "I do not intend to let the matter drop because vital principles are at stake."

The following month reference was made again to the silence of Richard Richards, who surfaced at last in the April issue. In a lengthy letter which explained that he had at all times given Foster the credit due, he placed the blame wholly and entirely on the slim shoulders of Culbertson. He added: "I feel that not only should the *Bridge World* apologize to you both by letter and in their magazine, but that they owe me an apology also."

This explanation was graciously accepted by the mollified author, but from Culbertson not a word until the following month, when in an article as momentous as the Ems telegram Manning-Foster let slip the dogs of war.

As no précis could reproduce the style of Albert Edye at his polemical best, and as this momentous declaration deserves a tardy resurrection from the archives of history, it is here reproduced in full:

CULBERTSON SYSTEM OF ETHICS IN JOURNALISM

Stealing an author's literary wares is not so serious a crime as baby-snatching or rum-running. All the same it is an offence and to prevent it there are copyright laws which are recognised in all civilised countries.

Mr. Ely Culbertson apparently is ignorant of the existence of such laws, or if he is not, he thinks they should be defied.

That at any rate is the plain meaning of an article in his organ entitled: 'Much ado about Nothing', referring to the Richards case.

So far as Mr. Richards is concerned, the matter is closed. He has made his explanation.

But Mr. Culbertson cannot be let off so lightly. Instead of a frank public apology for his infringement of copyright, he is merely impertinent to me.

The burden of his article, reinforced by a quotation from Kipling, is that every author steals and to object is to make 'Much Ado about Nothing'.

Mr. Culbertson's offence is aggravated in that in the course of his article he makes two absolutely untrue statements.

He alleges that 'in recent books' I have 'borrowed liberally' from his writings.

This is entirely false. First of all I have published no books since Mr. Culbertson produced his first book in 1930, and my own new book just published contains no extracts from his writings. To avoid quibble, and in case he should say he means not books but articles, I would add that with regard to them the statement is equally inaccurate. I had written many books and hundreds of articles on Bridge before Mr. Culbertson was ever heard of.

The second mis-statement is that 'Some of the very finest things appearing in *Bridge Magazine* were originally printed in the *Bridge World*.'

The *Bridge Magazine* was founded in May, 1926, and the *Bridge World* in October, 1929.

We managed to exist without the help of Mr. Culbertson's organ for over three years!

By an arrangement with him, it was agreed that we might reproduce articles from his magazine and he might reproduce articles from ours. I have availed myself very sparingly of the arrangement. Indeed, I have so much good matter, that I have found room for less than a dozen articles from the *Bridge World* in the course of over two years, and these most certainly are not our 'very finest things'.

In fact the suggestion that as an author or an Editor I depend in any way at all upon Mr. Culbertson or his magazine for inspiration, is grotesquely untrue, and he only renders himself ridiculous by making it.

The honeymoon was over. The Rubicon crossed. It was war to the knife.

As this month was the sixth anniversary of the magazine, he called on Mrs. Edith Sefi, the laureate of Kensington, whose muse was, as ever, on tap for a good cause.

She came up with the following lyric, which combined the felicities of a birthday greeting with the fervors of a battle-hymn:

> Should you ask me why this verse is?
> I should answer: I should tell you
> For the Magazine's sixth birthday;
> For the honour of its Founder.
> In the lovely month of May-time,
> When the May trees all are budding,
> Comes the Magazine to cheer us,
> For the sixth year, comes to cheer us.
> You shall hear how Manning-Foster
> Started on its publication:
> Not for triumph in the battle;
> Not for self and not for glory,
> But for profit of the people;
> For advantage of all players.
> As unto the bow the cord is,
> So to readers is this Journal.
> As we read it, we obey it;
> Many teachings do we follow;
> Useless we without its guidance.

It had probably never occurred to Culbertson until then that he was stirring up a hornets' nest, or for that matter that his hitherto complaisant English ally would turn out to be a hornet. In fact, it is doubtful if he wrote the "Much Ado About Nothing" article at all, because after the Lenz match he had a great deal to do in radio, films, lecture tours, and so on. That is irrelevant, however. As he would say himself, he was the fall guy, and his despised opponent, with an unlooked for Machiavellism brought the war to his very doorstep in New York.

The British Bridge League was founded in May 1931 in circumstances unprecedented since Louis Quatorze made his immortal proclamation *"L'état c'est moi."* At least when Mr. R. R.
Richards founded the American Bridge League in 1927 he was
conventional enough to have a committee present. No such
tedious formality impeded the accouchement of its British
counterpart which took place in the editorial sanctum of the
Bridge Magazine. But let Manning-Foster describe the happy
event in his own inimitable way:

Accordingly, at a packed meeting consisting of myself, my
Sub-Editor and a black cat for luck, the League was formally
inaugurated on May 1st., and I was unanimously elected Hon.
President, and my Sub-Editor Hon. Secretary with power to
add to our number!

Now, why do I take all this trouble? I am not a whole-
hearted philanthropist, although I am prepared to do a good
turn for others when I can.

First of all, let me say there is no idea of making money out
of the scheme. I believe in starting it I am doing a Boy Scout's
good Action of the day.

The League, starting so improbably from an overall membership of one, became an immediate success, and in next to no
time had a membership extending to every corner of what was
still the Empire. Clearly the appeal of a Boy Scout who didn't
even charge a bob was irresistible! At the same time, Manning-
Foster, who would rank very high in anybody's list of the world's
worst bridge experts, was an excellent organizer. One is tempted
to put him right up in the Culbertson class; he was almost of
this caliber, but not quite, as he was in time to find out.

In the meantime, his antagonist having other and more pressing trans-Atlantic preoccupations, the way was open to him to
extend his tentacles.

Now the British was by no means the first of the national
associations. As far back as 1929 the Austrians had formed their

Bridge Union, later known as Federation; this was followed in 1930 by the Netherland Bridge League and the Indian Bridge Association. Early in 1931 Canada, Australia, and Hungary followed suit, so when Manning-Foster assumed the mantle of Baden-Powell he was following a well-trodden trail. In fact, in 1931 a European tournament, the first of its kind, sponsored by the Dutch League was held at the Hague, but it had no official status. Nor had its successor in June 1932 at Scheveningen, under the same auspices. At that tournament, however, on June 7 the European Bridge League was formed, the founder members being Austria, Belgium, England, France, Germany, Holland, Hungary and Norway. It need hardly he added that the first President was Albert Edye Manning-Foster.

At the end of 1932, therefore, our hero was beginning to feel his muscles, for the European League had by now the accretion of the membership of Czechoslovakia, Denmark, Italy, Portugal and Switzerland. But the thunderclouds were gathering on the horizon.

Already during that year, mainly as a counterblast to the American Bridge League which hated his guts and said so, but also with a piercing stare at the European goings-on of his erstwhile ally, Mr. Foster, Culbertson formed the National Bridge Association of America with its headquarters in his own New York offices. Having defeated the Official System. Culbertson's adherents were numbered by the millions so that the effect of this Cromwellian *coup d'état* was to put a stranglehold on Bridge administration in the United States. Soon the older American Bridge League was gasping for breath. In its extremity it turned to the European League, with the result that while preserving their domestic autonomy, the two leagues merged to become the International Bridge League. This development Mr. Culbertson took nonchalantly in his stride, and under his benediction and with the help of his *fidus Achates,* Hubert Phillips, there was formed the National Bridge Association of Great Britain. At the same time the *British Bridge World* magazine was founded under Phillips's editorship to spread the gospel.

This publication, which lasted until 1939, made practically no impact on the public, perhaps because being quite an intelligent production it lacked the cloud cuckoo-land atmosphere of its distinguished contemporary, although it also had the good fortune to have the backing of a huge firm of playing-card manufacturers. It did, however, have the intended effect of adding an additional dash of gall to the wormwood cocktail which Mr. Culbertson was in the process of shaking for the newly inaugurated president of the European Bridge League.

So far from observing the usual journalistic courtesies, which he so trenchantly upheld in l'affaire Richards-Culbertson, never once in the seven years of its lifetime did Manning-Foster allow, by even the most oblique reference, the chaste columns of his magazine to be profaned by an acknowledgement of the existence of its upstart rival.

This majestic detachment did not, naturally, apply to either Mr. Culbertson or his British and American associations, and although most of 1933 foreshadowed a later phoney war, there was a considerable amount of firing at extreme range. For instance, we find in an editorial, dark with foreboding, in February of that year, under the by-line "Gangster Tactics," "There is at least one organization which while masquerading under the name British is of American origin." This disclosure was presumably so damnatory as to require no further comment. It does, however, go on to add *apropos* the tactics of the architects of this unmentionable combination, "One can only stand amazed at their profound ignorance and meaningless effrontery." It was only poetic justice that the author of the sentiments was in time to stand and surrender to these very tacticians, on terms, admittedly, but terms sued for by himself.

Two inflammatory events led to the outbreak of the real shooting war which broke out in November. These were the first European Championships held under the auspices of the newly formed European Bridge League at Grosvenor House in May and June, and the Beasley-Culbertson Match at Selfridges the following month.

As can well be imagined the former event under the presidency of Manning-Foster was conducted in accordance with a protocol of gentility which might have been ordained by the Widow of Windsor herself. The contestants, representative of Austria, Belgium, Denmark, England, Holland and Norway, were received at the Guildhall by the Lord Mayor. A dizzy round of pleasure was laid on including a visit to Epsom to see the immortal Hyperion win the Derby, and another to a session of the World Economic Conference which, not inappropriately, was housed in the Natural History Museum in South Kensington.

At the end of the week a banquet was held with the president in the chair. The *pièce de resistance* was the speech of a German guest who, paying tribute to the president, stressed the atmosphere of fraternal goodwill engendered by international intercourse, such a happy augury for world peace. This, in the year of the accession of Adolf H. Schickelgruber, was a source of great reassurance to the delegates of the various nationalities, and particularly to the Austrian, whose team had won the European title.

It is painful to have to chronicle that one discordant note intruded on this auspicious harmony. It passes all understanding that even Manning-Foster should have had the childlike innocence to invite Ely Culbertson to this tournament in the role of observer, having as good as described him as an American gangster a couple of months previously. Possibly he was under the impression that the conventional behavior of guest towards host would induce Mr. C. to seize the hand of friendship so generously offered.

In one way he was correct, he did seize it—between his teeth. In an interview which was prominently featured in the newspapers of two continents Mr. Culbertson gave his considered opinion of the bidding and play, which was not calculated to affect the contestants with any delusions of grandeur. He amplified these observations with a reference to the arrangements for the tournament itself, which he suspected had been

99

delegated to a clergyman's wife with a wide experience of running whist drives in the parish hall. He took this opportunity of contrasting them unfavorably with his own preparations for the forthcoming Beasley match, and added that it was supererogatory to restrict spectators to ticket holders as no one in his senses would go to the Grosvenor House contest anyway.

This clinical appraisal was hardly balm to the soul of Albert Edye, particularly the bit about the arrangements which were specifically in his bailiwick, nor was his anguish assuaged by the contemplation of the horde of disappointed spectators in Oxford Street who could not obtain admittance to the match for the Schwab Trophy.

If anything were required to exacerbate him further, this historic encounter supplied it, and he reacted with unwonted speed, if characteristic ineptitude.

His first effort proved to be a very damp squib indeed. It has been noted that one of Culbertson's motives in playing Beasley was to publicize his latest brainchild, the 4-5 No Trump slam convention. There is no doubt that this was a first class idea as it undoubtedly brought some kind of precision to hitherto slap-dash methods; thirty years later it is still part of the armory of many of the world's leading players. There is equally no doubt that it is strictly a convention for good players, and in the hands of the unskilled can be very much a double-edged weapon, and in all probability for every slam bid won by its use, twice as many games have been lost by its misuse.

This factor Mr. Foster chose to ignore, and with an eye on injuring his antagonist in his Achilles heel—the sales of his book—he roundly condemned it as a form of cheating to which no honest player would descend. In this denunciation, wonderful to relate, he found an improbable ally in his ancient enemy, Colonel Buller; love and war make for strange bed-fellows. Between the pair of them they induced the Portland Club to declare the convention illegal, with unlooked for results, because the proscription by that august body had roughly the same effect on the bridge-playing public as the label "Banned in Ireland" has on the sales of the choicer offerings of book shops in Charing Cross Road.

It should be added that the New York Whist Club displayed rather more good sense in refusing to act as unpaid agents for the Culbertson system, and dealt with Manning-Foster's importunities in a very effective way by ignoring them.

His other attempt at sabotage dates back a little further to the previous year, when, having contemplated with growing distress the sales of his own books which were in inverse proportion to those of Culbertson's, he decided to retrieve his fortunes with a game of his own invention, on which he wrote a book.

This monstrosity, the offspring of a shotgun marriage between Bridge and Plafond, he christened ingeniously Bridge-Plafond. He announced that this would remedy the deplorable condition into which Contract Bridge had sunk, because of the commercialism and sensationalism of certain interests which with gentlemanly reticence he did not name.

Every month the public was assured that the sales of this book were booming, and in December he was in a position to announce, "Bridge-Plafond *will* be the game of the future." The event fell somewhat short of this prophecy; indeed the literary historian searches for the beauties of this pastime with the same frustration as the scholar for the lost odes of Sappho, or the philologist for the secrets of the Etruscan language. Not even the British Museum can produce a single copy. Perhaps the true explanation is that these same sinister interests bought up and destroyed every volume!

Be that as it may, what is quite clear is that his antagonist throughout this embattled year seems to have treated the twin threats of Bridge-Plafond, and the banning of his convention, with an infuriating equanimity. Manning-Foster, however, felt that, come what may, he always had his Bridge League from which Culbertson and all his works and pomps had been exorcised, or so he fondly thought until in November 1933 came the bombshell.

As it would be presumptuous to attempt to paraphase the manly prose of the affronted president, he must be allowed to express his honest indignation in his own way:

CULBERTSON'S REPLY TO INTERNATIONAL BRIDGE LEAGUE

The antics of Mr. Ely Culbertson are amazing and amusing. His reply to the ban of the International Bridge League on his tournaments and the refusal of the American Bridge League to recognise his rights to represent America is the establishment of an 'International Contract Bridge Union' grandiloquently described as a World Wide, Official, Non-Partisan, Non-Profit Making Organisation of National Bridge Leagues and Organisations.

At the time of writing it consists of a recently established Association Francaise de Bridge-Contract de Paris, The National Bridge Association of Great Britain, and The U.S. Bridge Association of New York.

It aims at ousting and superseding the well organised federation of the leagues of 12 countries. Any Association which applies for membership must agree not to belong to any other International Association or Bridge League.

We are asked to cable at the new Association's expense the one word 'Yes' if we should be interested in joining! The British Bridge League, in common I believe with all the 12 leagues affiliated to the International Bridge League, has saved the new Union that expense.

The fact that the newly formed Natonal Bridge Association of Great Britain has allied itself with this organization speaks for itself.

If players believe that this new 'Union' will promote their

real interests they will believe anything. There is much more to it than meets the eye at first sight.

Despite the truly Christian tone of Manning-Foster's Christmas editorial which was headed "Peace on Earth Goodwill towards Men; Bridge is a Game," Mr. Culbertson's audacious demarche fomented a war which split international Bridge right down the middle for more than three years.

8

War and Peace

It was not by chance that the war of the Leagues and Associations coincided with the rise of Duplicate Bridge. By the early thirties the professors had become joyfully and fiercely aware that success in this form of the game represented big money in terms of the sales of books and syndicated articles, as well as radio, films, and all the other grist that came to the mills of the winners of major tournaments. If the winner happened to be playing a system which he had devised himself, he could call any bank manager his friend. It was also not the least of their achievements that they succeeded in persuading a great number of players in the U.S.A. that this variation was the most enjoyable. In those far distant and more courtly days they may well have been right.

As one might expect, while Culbertson was not the first to appreciate and learn this financial fact of life, he was the first to exploit it in the grand manner.

When Vanderbilt invented Contract as we know it in 1925 the conditions for its rapid spread were already present in the United States. After Mitchell and Howell had discovered their respective methods of determining the winners of pairs playing identical hands the success of Duplicate Whist in that country was immediate. As we know, Auction Bridge was soon to oust the older game with the result that shortly after the

104

first world war Duplicate Auction was already widely played.

When Contract became the rage it took possession of a field well prepared for it, and the result was dynamic. It is true to say that there is no precedent in any other sphere of recreation for the phenomenal rise of this game. Almost overnight Auction Bridge became old hat, and so much so that the revered *Auction Bridge Magazine,* edited by no less an authority than Milton Work, published its last regretful issue as early as September 1929.

By that time the American Bridge League was running its national tournaments for pairs and teams of four. There were Inter-State and Inter-City challenges and championships with that sort of indigenous publicity accorded to Babe Ruth's home runs, or the more spectacular exploits of Al Capone. As far back as 1923 E. V. Shephard had broadcast Auction, and now the big radio networks climbed on the bandwagon. Practically every newspaper carried a bridge column, written by its own pet expert, a title which was easier to obtain than to justify. In this regard it is perhaps sufficient to point out that by the end of 1933 more than six thousand books had been written on Contract Bridge. One wonders what has become of them.

The result was pure chaos, and were it not for Culbertson there can be little doubt that the game would have expired from malnutrition.

But Culbertson, as we know, did arrive in the middle of this bedlam, and despite all his showmanship and charlatanry he did lay down the fundamental principles which underlie every successful system to the present day. He did a great deal more: by asserting these principles in his *Blue Book,* and publicizing them in his historic matches he ensured the widespread growth of Duplicate, and as a direct result a public and permanent interest in Contract Bridge which entitles it to the status of a social institution.

By 1929 almost the whole of Europe was in the grip of the new craze with the exception, oddly enough, of France, which was still chauvinistically faithful to her native game of Plafond; and, of course, England.

In September of that year Manning-Foster announced: "Those who prophesied that it would supersede Auction have been proved wrong." With a sideswipe at the ladies ". . . it is undoubtedly very popular with women . . ." He continues: "The idea that Contract gives such an advantage to the better player does not seem to be confirmed. On the contrary, it is the verdict of some of the best Bridge players that it is a less intellectual game than Auction . . ." It is charitable to comment that if these players were introduced to the game through the medium of the book Manning-Foster wrote their conclusion was entirely warranted.

If any further endorsement of these pronouncements was required it was supplied by no less an authority than The Thunderer itself. In an article about this time, a writer in *The Times* informs us:

> Men who are not, and never would be, first-class Auction players can hold their own in the best of company at Contract, the truth apparently being that a certain robust combination of common sense and audacity is more important than any card-playing skill. . . . Contract seems more suited to the American temperament than the British.

It is a pity that editorial tradition protects the anonymity of the scribe who cast these pearls less than a year before Culbertson turned English bridge inside out. In a way he deserves the same immortality as Chamberlain achieved when he informed the nation that "Hitler has missed the bus."

It will have been gathered that Duplicate Bridge was unknown in England at that time. Its hour, however, was at hand, and it came with the Buller-Culbertson match. This contest marked not only the foundation of Culbertson's personal fortune, but also that of Duplicate as an abiding and ever-increasing influence on the development and spread of Contract.

Now, it is easy to see why the abnormal and high pressure publicity attending the Buller match excited an immediate interest in this form of the game. The reasons for its sustained popularity among the general run of players are more subtle.

Somerset Maugham, a bridge addict himself, in a most untypical passage, wrote that the successful bridge player should be "truthful, clear-headed, considerate and prudent; these are also the essentials for the more important game of Life." It is saddening to see the master of cynicism dipping his pen in golden syrup. Perhaps the game has an unsettling effect on the mental processes.

Whatever Mr. Maugham's desiderata, and sound as two of them may be, certainly any aspiring bridge player who followed his benign advice of truthfulness and consideration at the bridge table would be an odds-on bet to finish in last place in the Christian Mothers' annual pairs tournament at Nether Wallop. It is certainly hard to believe that Mr. Maugham has ever played Duplicate.

Indeed, one imagines that if that acute observer had played in tournament bridge to any great extent he would have come to the conclusion that its continued success can be largely ascribed to its appeal to practically everyone of the baser human instincts.

Lest the last observation appear extravagant a brief glance at the motives which impel its devotees to play, think, talk and live duplicate bridge year in and year out should justify it.

It is not without significance that the Fathers of the Church placed Pride at the head of the list of the Seven Deadly Sins. It is unlikely that either St. Augustine of St. Thomas had Duplicate Bridge in mind when cataloguing this enormity, but certainly it could have given them a fruitful subject for a series of premonitory sermons, for no other product of human ingenuity has given the ordinary man greater and cheaper opportunities to indulge in a vanity he is otherwise compelled to disguise.

Another factor which played no small part in popularizing the game was its cheapness. Up to that time Bridge was almost exclusively an upper-class activity, and a fairly expensive one at that. Anyone who played a session at the usual stakes in any of the better London clubs might find himself embarrassed at the end of the evening if he had less than twenty-five pounds in his wallet, and at a pound per hundred—a common enough stake—he might need three times as much. In the era of the world depression this was as far beyond the means of the middle classes as the millionaires' table at Monte Carlo. If this were true of the men, it was very much more so of the women who, with more time on their hands if their husbands had the good fortune to be in employment, accounted for more than 75 per cent of the bridge-playing population, as they still do.

Now, for half a crown or so these people could play in tournaments every night of their lives, and a great number of them did. It was naturally in the interests of teachers and bridge clubs to promote these tournaments, so that there was soon hardly a town in the country that had not at least one bridge match every week. A measure of the upsurge of the game can be found in the entry of more than four thousand from all over the country for the National Pairs Championship of 1934, and this represented an entry of those who presumably were the best players.

But Duplicate had a more far-reaching effect on the future of Contract. Taking the sales of Culbertson's *Blue Book* and relating them to the number of Duplicate players, it can be estimated roughly that by the middle thirties they represented about one player in fifty. But this figure bears no relationship to the interest aroused, as the scenes at the Beasley match in 1933 testify.

Another side effect of competitive bridge was the confounding of the masterminds at least one of whom every golf and social club suffered from. The hours of these tyrants were now numbered. If they were ill-advised enough to play in competitions they now found it hard to explain away a losing contract in no trumps when everyone else had made game in spades on the same cards. If they did not, they were certain to find themselves the victims of inquisitions by partners who did play duplicate, which if they made for greater efficiency represented an unfortunate decline in amity, and which found frequent and pungent expression in post mortems often lasting longer than the actual playing of the hand.

Unfortunately, however, the eclipse of these self-appointed pundits created a vacuum which was filled by practically everybody who had read a bridge book. This also led to preliminary cross-examinations on the particular form of insanity to which partner subscribed. In the early days this often gave rise to an acrimony which blighted many a budding friendship, nowadays although the cross-examinations continue, the effects are not so serious, as it is now axiomatic that every strange partner is a lunatic, as is every opponent a cheat. It is a matter of hard fact that while every partner misplays the hand, the player himself does not make a mistake—he takes what he euphemistically describes as a "view."

Thanks to Culbertson the Buller match sparked off an intense public interest and the very next year were initiated two major competitions, the Gold Cup for teams of four, and the National Paris Championship. Both competitions were founded by the British Bridge League, which shortly afterwards sponsored the Whitelaw Cup for women.

While the trophies for these competitions were, and are, the most coveted prizes in English Bridge, a great number of other tournaments sprang up all over Britain, quite unconnected with the Bridge League. A number of counties, regions, and cities formed their own associations and ran their own tournaments, and held congresses at which it was possible to win quite valuable prizes.

In the popularizing of such events by far the greatest influence was that of Hubert Phillips, the Editor of *British Bridge World*. It is no exaggeration to describe him as the father of Duplicate Bridge in England. He was largely responsible for the arrangements for the Buller match, and as a result became a life-long devotee of the Culbertson system. The extent of this evangelism may be gauged from the fact that he captained the *Bridge World* teams at various congresses, and founded the English Bridge Union, the Duplicate Bridge Control Board, and the London and Home Counties Association, none of which activities endeared him to Mr. Albert Edye Manning-Foster.

Another phenomenon that owes its genesis to the Buller contest is the challenge match. The Colonel himself was the first in the field, but he was soon followed by a number of others eager to mine this vein. A series of friendly and not so friendly challenges ensued, and soon there were matches between North and South, London and the Provinces, and so on. So popular were these jousts with the public that a challenge match between Crockfords Club and teams from Germany and Holland received nearly as much newspaper coverage as the Buller match itself.

This new vogue was meat and drink to Buller, who embarked on a series of matches in pretty well every city in the British Isles. With the pickings, and all expenses paid in the best hotels, this was great fun and profitable too. Furthermore, these encounters were made doubly enjoyable by the fact that he always won them. Every victory was claimed as a victory for British Bridge, as distinct from playing skill, and at the post-prandial conviviality which inevitably followed each encounter, he always paid his hosts this delicate compliment. In return, as often as not, they proceeded to buy his books. In fact, the exact opposite was the truth. Buller won because he and his teammates, who often included Ewart Kempson, a really magnificent player, were all first class performers, whereas the provincial opposition were invariably mere tyros at that time; for a few years Buller was shrewd enough not to cross swords with the experts.

In the Spring of 1934 his triumphal gallop came to a sudden

and catastrophic stop in circumstances which would have rejoiced the heart of the mischievous Ely himself.

After the Anglo-American match the Colonel produced a book in which he modestly pointed out that of the eight players his was by far the outstanding performance. In a detailed special pleading which he described as an analysis of the hands played he roundly claimed the match to be a complete vindication of his theories, and a complete success for British Bridge.

For anyone indelicate enough to point to the actual result he had a crushing reply. The English defeat was solely due to the ineptitude of his teammates, whom he politely characterized as a "collection of third-raters," two of whom "proceeded to under-call in an incredible fashion throughout the proceedings." One of the recipients of these gracious compliments was Cedric Kehoe, who became doubly the object of Buller's choler when he became a convert to the Culbertson System. Mr. Kehoe, who was an Irishman, had the Irish memory for ancient wrongs, and he did not forget—for nearly four long years.

At last, and the precise date must be recorded for in a way it was historic, on March 27 and 28, 1934, a team from Almacks, captained by Kehoe and playing Culbertson, met Buller playing British Bridge.

In the history of Contract Bridge, before or since, never was a sweeter or more devastating revenge exacted. Kehoe not merely beat Buller, he scientifically and systematically immolated him, and when the massacre mercifully ended there was nothing left but to sweep up the remains of British Bridge which metaphorically strewed the floor of the Dorchester where the butchery took place.

In an interview with the press Kehoe summed it up: "British Bridge committed suicide. Our opponents required no beating, they beat themselves." It was the death-knell of British Bridge.

The Colonel, in fact, went far to justify the proverb that old soldiers never die. As late as 1936, he pleaded rather pathetically "British Bridge has not failed, it has simply not been tried." In May 1938 he faded away.

111

Poor old Buller, he certainly enlivened the English scene, and just as certainly we shall not gaze upon his like again.

In the meanwhile the war of the associations continued on both sides of the Atlantic, including the Continent. It would be tedious to follow it throughout its vagaries, but some of its effects were diverting. For instance, in America, from the early days of tournament bridge, a system had been devised for grading the abilities of the players, by analogy with Chess. This took the form of awarding Master Points to players who had distinguished themselves in competitive play.

The hierarchy of this green baize aristocracy ranged all the way from Life Masters, through National Masters down to Junior Masters, who had the privilege of lording it over the pointless hoipolloi on their native heaths. It should be noted *en passant* that the female of Master is Master.

This is a very arbitrary way of determining a player's skill, and it has been well said that while a Life Master cannot be a really bad player, he does not have to be really good. At the same time it became the burning ambition of the fanatic tournament players to collect as many master points as they could, and at the present time in the United States it is by no means unusual for competitors to fly three thousand miles in quest of these dubious status symbols.

Mr. Ogden Nash finds the apotheosis of snobbery manifested in the game of golf, and in immortal verse informs us:

> The Hollywood snob will look you through
> And stalk back into his clique,
> For he knows that he is better than you
> By a couple of grand a week;
> And the high-caste Hindu's fangs are bared
> If a low-caste Hindu blinks;
> But they're just like one of the boys, compared
> To the nabobs of the links.

In turn, Mr. Nash should be informed that these social interchanges are democratic compared with the supercilious scorn of a Life Master for a Senior Master, or either for a Junior Master who, if he knows his proper place, retires to a sort of social ghetto at any well conducted bridge congress.

The allotting of master points was exclusively within the province of the American Bridge League, and everything in this monopolistic and lucrative garden was lovely until the row with Culbertson started.

When he set up his United States Bridge Association it also proceeded to award master points which, while it added to the fun, rather tended to debase the coinage. Harmony was not to be brought into chaos until the general peacemaking which took place in 1937, when both sides sank their differences and the American Contract Bridge League was born.

Probably Culbertson's most ingenious and successful tour de force was his promotion of a universal tournament for bridge players to be held in 1932, the year of the Olympic Games. According, he announced in the June 1931 issue of the *Bridge World,* a "World Championship Contract Tournament to be played at the same hour in every country throughout the world." The particulars appeared in all the leading papers and bridge magazines, and the response exceeded even the most sanguine expectations of the promoter. It also, very naturally, improved the look of his bank balance because of the two dollar entry fee per player, one was payable into the coffers of the National Bridge Association, alias Mr. Ely Culbertson, and although the figures have never been published it is estimated that there were nearly a million entrants.

A few excerpts from the announcement explain the scheme and display the highly individual literary style of the master:

WORLD TOURNAMENT OF A MILLION PLAYERS
GIGANTIC AMERICAN SCHEME

Briefly the plan is this, Sixteen hands will be prepared by Mr. and Mrs. Ely Culbertson. On sealed slips, the contents of which will be sacredly guarded, will be recorded the correct bidding and the correct play. At the chosen hour, in every city in the world, those entering the contest will be given the hands in specially designed boards.

It may be observed in parenthesis that 'the chosen hour' was 8 p.m., New York time on April 1, 1932, which meant that in Europe play began at 1 a.m. and continued until well after dawn.

Mr. Culbertson proceeds:

This tournament is unique in that while each player is competing with the world's masters, he will do so under the most favorable conditions. He will actually be playing with the person with whom he is accustomed to meet daily at the Bridge table. Thus, the player, will have an opportunity to compete with par unawed by the reputation of his opponent and unaffected by strange surroundings.

At this point the author himself becomes over-awed in the contemplation of his own genius, and achieves a passage of high lyricism:

Through this competition a dream of civilization will be realized. At one particular hour and extending for several hours, people of all races and languages will be speaking the one universal language—that of Bridge.

One would have thought that participation in the realization of this Utopia would be its own reward, but more mundane inducements were held out, presumably for the mercenary minority. These were gold cups and other booty including automobiles and free trips to and from Europe.

At all events, the idea was so spectacularly successful that it was repeated every year until the war, and has been continued in one form or another ever since. It also conferred a cachet on Culbertson's Association which gave him no less gratification than profit.

A farcical situation also developed in England, where there was no governing body with exclusive jurisdiction over tournament Bridge. Manning-Foster, on behalf of the Bridge League, disdained even to recognize the existence of the various associations, and in particular the Culbertson-inspired British Bridge Association, which were successfully running innumerable tournaments under his nose. So far did this judicial, if injudicious, detachment go that in the summer of 1936 he announced that he would have nothing to do with the English Bridge Union, despite the fact that this organization picked the teams and ran the contests between the four home countries for the Camrose Trophy. He also thought fit to inform the Duplicate Bridge Control Board, whose leading lights included such outstanding figures as Richard Lederer, Kenneth Konstam and Graham Mathieson, that he knew nothing about it, or its affiliated leagues.

This ostrich-like nonsense, however, had to stop sometime, and at a meeting in Paris in October 1936 the articles were drawn up for a treaty of peace on the international front. There was to be one International Bridge League, with which was merged Culbertson's International Contract Bridge Union. This body was to control all international bridge affairs, and comprised a European and an American division, the president to be American and European alternately. It was also announced that the first official world championship would be held at Budapest the following June, for which Culbertson magnanimously presented the trophy.

The delegates left Paris in an atmosphere of peace above all earthly dignities.

This fraternal harmony spread to the United States, and the following October Culbertson in a touching passage charged with honest emotion, in announcing the merger of the American Bridge League and the U.S. Bridge Association, wrote—"Let us forget the past, and go forward together, having obliterated all traces of petty jealousies, grudges, and differences of opinion."

115

Henceforth there was to be the American Contract Bridge League, which when it assimilated the Pacific League had exclusive jurisdiction. The rankings of the players were re-organized under one system of Master Points.

For a while it was otherwise in England where Manning-Foster still led the old guard in a rearguard action. Not until 1938 did the North Eastern Association, founded by Ewart Kempson, and oldest of all, become affiliated. A letter about this time informed Hubert Phillips that the Duplicate Board of Control could not be recogized, nor could the National Bridge Union, the forerunner of the English Bridge Union.

At the beginning of 1939, however, Manning-Foster resigned as president of the Bridge League in favour of Sir Noel Mobbs, and he continued as editor of the *Bridge Magazine* in name only. The January issue dropped Auction Bridge from its cover for the first time.

There was now no obstacle to an alliance, and largely as a result of the efforts of Noel Mobbs for the League, and Geoffrey Butler for the Union, a permanent and sensible *rapprochement* was achieved. Broadly speaking, the latter looks after all regional associations, home internationals and tournaments and the League, to which it is affiliated, deals with European and world tournaments and matters of international government.

Manning-Foster never knew that the September issue of his magazine would be the last to appear under his editorial name. In fact, it would be the last to appear for a decade and it carried his obituary, for he died on August 28, 1939. On the day of his funeral Adolf Hitler invaded Poland, and the old order changed with spectacular suddenness.

9

Along the Briny Beach

It has been estimated by an eminent authority, who had obviously nothing better to do, that the normal bridge session involves the average player in four hundred borderline decisions, one in three of which he will make incorrectly. This entails an incidence of 133.3 recurring critical strictures per partner per session, which is exactly the figure most conscientious workers in this field will arrive at, particularly in regard to the recurring part.

This statistic we are told relates to modern standards, which should be a source of consolation to the middle-aged average player who can congratulate himself that it was not based on the egregious bidding and play with which he profaned the bridge tables in the prewar decade. The difference between his performance now and then is that whereas he now continues to repeat the same mistakes with clockwork regularity, in the days of his youth he added a new one to his repertoire practically every time he sat down to play. And small blame to him; when one considers the handicaps under which he labored it is bordering on the miraculous that he ever played the correct card, or made the proper bid.

Bridge players of that era fell into two categories. They were either converts from Auction, or else had been taught Contract by players whose knowledge of the basic principles was sketchy.

In either case their plight was an unhappy one, as the score sheets of the average rubbers would testify had they been preserved for posterity. What have, in fact, been preserved are the records of the matches between the experts, where we find penalties of eighteen hundred points were as common as leaves in Autumn. We are therefore in a position to judge the caliber of the run-of-the-mill players when we look at the terrifying results achieved by their betters.

Further instructive evidence is supplied by the spate of books inflicted on the defenseless public at this period, each advocating what its author euphemistically described as his "system." None of these alleged systems had anything in common with any other except a denominator of fallacy. The bewilderment of the unfortunate neophytes found expression in the queries they addressed to the Readers' Bureau of the *Bridge Magazine,* which ran monthly into several pages. It is difficult to say which was the more astonishing, the naiveté of the questions, or the fatuity of the replies. While that department makes for entertaining reading nowadays, to reflect on the mistakes which it disseminated sobers us again.

All this insanity naturally infected tournament bridge, and except when the players were selected on known ability, pairs tournaments became farcical and no test of merit whatever. And if this were true of pairs contests it was doubly so of individual championships where each competitor had to play at least two hands with every other entrant. The results were so horrifying or diverting, depending on whether one was the victim or the beneficiary, that this was the period par excellence of the snide wisecracks by outraged partners, some of which have become part of the folklore of the game wherever it is played.

For instance, George S. Kaufman, who in between writing Broadway successes made himself a top-class bridge player, found himself partnering a strange lady in an individual tournament. When she proceeded to massacre an apparently cast-iron contract Kaufman inquired:

"Madam, when did you take up this game? Oh! I know it was today, but what time today?"

In similar circumstances at a big Chicago tournament an irate female delivered such an attack on her partner that the unfortunate delinquent ran from the table in the general direction of the bar, leaving a pair of very embarrassed opponents behind him. Eventually, one of them in a misguided effort at light conversation asked:

"Are you married to that gentleman?"
to receive the reply:

"God help me, of course I am. Do you think I'd live in sin with a half-witted oaf who plays his cards like that?"

Perhaps the most helpful advice was given by an onlooker at a major tournament. When one of the contestants asked him, "How should I have played that last hand?" it was suggested, "Under an assumed name."

In England, where the fundamentals of the game were even more imperfectly assimilated, confusion was endemic. It is not surprising that some of the better players with analytical minds decided to do something about it. Hence the evolution of the Acol system of bidding upon which Britain's future Bridge fortunes were soundly based. In any other country it would be paradoxical that a system which is now regarded as distinctively British and peculiarly suited to the Anglo-Saxon genius should be the creation of a Russian immigrant who was born in Manchuria.

Simon Skidelsky was a man of many parts, who in his lifetime became as fanciful a legend in British Bridge as the immortal Buller himself. When he arrived in London via Dneipropetrovsk without any means of support immediately apparent to the naked eye, he not merely graduated with Honors from the London School of Economics, but he established himself under the name of S. J. Simon as a writer of some distinction. He collaborated in an excellent piece of spoof Shakesperian exegesis *No Bed for Bacon,* and was a contributor to such diverse publications as *Punch* and the *Economist* before

119

he found his true *metier* which was writing, living, expounding and, to an extent, creating Contract Bridge.

His personal eccentricities were Johnsonian, and as the great Panjandrum bestrewed himself with snuff, so "Skid" Simon moved in a nebula of cigarette ash, which he scattered with impartial abandon on his person and his friends.

The use of water for shaving or other external application he regarded as an effete affectation, and sartorially he was quite prepared to meet the world in frayed gray flannels and dinner jacket, as distinct from the sports coat which was reserved for formal occasions. He was no less idiosyncratic in his use of the English language which with him found a purer expression in authorship than in utterance. Terence Reese tells us that as long as he knew him he never heard him employ the definite article. He invariably referred to himself in the third person and, in addition to certain consonantal difficulties, spoke a peculiar form of telegraphese that could have ensured him a seat on the editorial board of *Time Magazine*.

This was the character who, with his great friend J. C. H. (Jack) Marx evolved the system which was to win every major prewar tournament in the country and eventually to bring Britain to six postwar European and one World Championship. They called it Acol for no better reason than that the two friends met in an obscure bridge club of that name in Acol Road, Hampstead, where they first discussed their theories on the game, and later developed them over gallons of black coffee and argument.

Of the system itself, it can be said that its appeal to the English temperament probably lies in the fact that it is as insusceptible of definition as the British constitution. Simon described it oracularly as "an attitude of mind," which at least complies with the Napoleonic dictum that the essence of every good constitution is vagueness.

The two theorists brought a wind of change to bear on the bridge confusion of the 1930's, for which players all over the world are indebted. If their functions can be allotted, the intuitive Simon may be described as the synthesist who propounded the theories, and Marx as the analyst who broke them down to their essential parts. While the basic principles were those that Culbertson had either determined or adopted, at the same time Acol applied them in some cases more flexibly, and in others, as for instance in no-trump bidding, more rigidly by using a point count method.

Although no book was published on the system until 1938, the gospel was spread by discussion and the success which attended the Acolites in tournaments.

Simon soon discovered Maurice Harrison-Gray and taught him to walk the sacred way to such effect that he was to represent Britain in more successful championships than any other player. Shortly afterwards, there was enlisted among the elect a young man called Iain Macleod who later captained a winning British team in 1950. It would have been a great affront to Simon's *amour propre* if he had lived to see the day his protegé allowed himself to be so far seduced from his responsibilities as to take over the job of leader of the House of Commons.

Another spectacular convert was Terence Reese who, in conjunction with Ben Cohen, popularized the system by collaborating in the first book on it in 1938. Reese originally subscribed to the Four Aces system and then became a disciple of Richard Lederer, whose book *Lederer Bids Two Clubs* was the lineal forebear of Acol and its systemic offshoots which are the distinctively British contributions to bridge. Through a natural process of evolution Reese adopted Acol, or more correctly, it adopted him, with conspicuously gratifying results for both the system and its convert who, in applying its methods with his partner, Boris Schapiro, formed probably the outstanding postwar partnership in the world.

Incidentally, the future apostles of Acol, Reese and Macleod, first met each other as rivals in the inaugural match between Oxford and Cambridge. Now an annual affair, it was initiated by Macleod who captained the other place which lost to Oxford whose captain was Reese.

Acol was first played in tournament bridge in 1933, but its triumphant progress really got under way a little later so that the records of the Gold Cup, and the National Pairs Championship, and most other major tournaments for the last four years of the decade show such continuous success for the system as almost to amount to a monopoly. It is, however, fair to reiterate that the system was merely an improved version of Culbertson. Its success owed a great deal more to the prowess of its exponents and their partnership *rapport* than to its own inherent virtues. Probably similar results would have crowned their efforts had they played Culbertson, plain and unadorned by their refinements.

It would be idle to suggest that these stirring activities had the least effect on those of the vast majority of bridge players. For their part, they fulfilled their destiny in a bottomless ocean of four thousand point rubbers with the fatalistic resignation of Norwegian lemmings. They were not merely the victims of their own invincible ignorance but, far worse, of the perplexing doctrines of those pundits who inspired Mrs. Sefi, the poetess, to cry "Many teachings do we follow."

When they turned to tournament bridge for relief from their losses, they found themselves persecuted even by the police who proscribed the Scarborough Summer Congress of 1934, invoking for the purpose an enactment of Henry the Eighth, designed by that mettlesome monarch for the promotion of the warlike pursuit of archery among his liege subjects. Fortunately, the statute received a more liberal interpretation in Eastbourne where it was presumably held that the practice of toxophily and contract bridge were not mutually exclusive undertakings. At all events, permission to hold it in that resort was granted, without, as far as is known, causing any permanent subversive injury to the state.

The London police as late as the middle forties decided that a seaside precedent was not binding on the metropolis, and, jealous of their country's safety, mounted an all-out offensive on the West End card clubs. This produced a typically abstruse piece of jurisprudence which laid down that Bridge, being a game in which skill predominates, is outside the Act, whereas Poker, being a gamble, is within it. It remains respectfully to submit that had the learned bench adjourned to any of the defendant clubs, it would have found that the direct contrary is the case.

In the United States, the average level was a great deal higher, although still far below the normal standards one would expect to find in an ordinary postwar club. This can be directly attributed to the single-mindedness the Americans devote to any game they take up, but above all to the influence of Ely Culbertson. The Culbertson System had so far overcome all opposition that from 1936 onwards it became the rule in tournament bridge that a partnership was called on to announce its system only if it were not playing Culbertson; this was also the practice, it should be added, everywhere else in the world other than in Britain and Europe. This is the more astonishing when one considers the size of the country, and the internecine strife between his Association and the League which, while ignoring the man, was forced to acknowledge his methods.

In this last connection it should be pointed out that there was an element of hoax in his describing his "methods" as the Culbertson System in the sense that they and it were proprietary articles. There is no doubt he was a first-class analyst and did make a great number of original contributions to the development of the game. It is equally true that he was a great eclecticist and had not the least compunction in appropriating the ideas of others when they had proved themselves.

For instance, the "principle of preparedness," which is that method of bidding designed to deal most effectively with partner's responses, was purloined from the Four Aces system, while the One Over One type of bidding, of which George Reith was the inventor, was similarly converted to his use and benefit. Both refinements appeared in his *Gold Book* without any disclosure of their sources. And these were only two of the unacknowledged debts which he amassed in the compilation of that opus.

The writings and theories of practically every bridge authority of any importance contributed to a greater or lesser degree, not least among them, as is not generally known, those of the now undeservedly forgotten James B. Elwell. Although not strictly a contract exponent, he deserves an honorable mention wherever the evolution of the game is discussed. As will later be seen, the manner of his departure from American bridge further earned the late Mr. Elwell a niche in its history to which the overworked adjective unique may properly be applied.

Culbertson's greatest achievement lay, therefore, in the correlation of his own with the sounder theories of others into a unified whole which he called his system. This was as much to the taste of bridge players as it was to their interest. Such was the strength of his organization, and so well had he indoctrinated his public, that a man could sit down for a game of contract with three strangers in a trans-continental train in the knowledge that all four were speaking the same bridge language. To this uniformity, more than anything else, may be ascribed the early arrival at bridge maturity of the ordinary American player as compared with his British counterpart, who in similar circumstances might have to attempt to adjust himself to three or four conflicting systems.

This very superiority of the Americans bred a complacency which so greatly impeded experiment and progress that in the decade preceding 1965 not once did they win the annual World Championship. In fact, their successful run lasted only from its resumption in 1950 until 1954. Since then the Italians have won it every year, except 1956 and 1960 when it went to France, and 1955 when Britain broke the American dominance. The signs, however, of an emergence from the wilderness are now present. European methods have been studied with rueful admiration, and overconfidence will certainly never again cause an American downfall.

On the European continent Contract became a craze even before it captured Britain, and the standard of play was incomparably higher. In Vienna and Budapest it was the highest in the world, as was the partnership of Jellenik and Schneider of Austria the best. In the seven official championships ending in 1939, Austria won three times, Hungary twice, and France and Sweden once each. The best Great Britain could do in that period was fourth, her average place in the table being fifth. The last three of these contests were for the World Championship which officially dates from 1937 when it was held in Budapest and won by Austria. This event was also memorable as it was the last appearance of Ely and Jo Culbertson on the world competitive scene as a partnership, maritally or otherwise, and the first of an unknown young protegée of his called Helen Sobel, who has been unchallenged ever since as the game's outstanding woman player.

The mention of this remarkable player introduces naturally a consideration of the effect of Contract Bridge upon her sex and vice versa. Of the thirty odd million players in the United States alone, it is estimated that at least 75 percent are women. Presumably, the statistics for other countries are similar because the pattern was the same from the beginning.

Whatever Mrs. Battle's tyranny at Whist, no counterpart of hers was to be found at the table in the early days of Bridge, if only for the reason that the game was played almost exclusively in clubs from which she was excluded, and regimental messes in which the mention of her name was not permitted. When Auction came along the position was slightly relaxed, but only slightly, and a woman bridge player was regarded by her fellows much as a woman cigar smoker is today.

The advent of Contract altered that almost overnight, and women everywhere, especially in America, took up the new game with an enthusiasm and ferocity that obliterated the last monastic bastion of the male.

It would have been surprising if Mr. Culbertson did not take that particular ball on the hop. He did, and a great deal more.

He made it almost a feminine reproach not to be able to play the game. In an unwonted burst of frankness he is on record for addressing a publicity organization on the methods he and Jo employed "to make the name Culbertson synonymous with contract bridge":

> We appealed to women, to their natural inferiority complex. Bridge was an opportunity for them to gain intellectual parity with their husbands. We worked on their fear instincts. We made it almost tantamount to shame not to play contract.
> I have sold bridge through sex—the game brought men and women together. I used the words "forcing bid" and "approach bid" because there is a connotation of sex to them.

Jo, of course, was a godsend to this campaign, and he built her up as the ideal player, superior to her husband in ability, cool, chic and immensely efficient withal. Thus was a legend contrived with diabolical cunning, and thus a looking glass in which every housewife saw with satisfaction her own superior image. Men in general, and husbands in particular, have paid a heavy price in the cause of this great illusion, as witness the martyrdom of John G. Bennett, late of Kansas City.

There is, however, an illusion about this illusion. It is certainly illusory to suggest, as did Ely, that a wife has a natural genius for the game, which is denied to her husband. In fact, the evidence is so much the other way as to permit no contradiction. Among the many superlative feminine qualities, and a curse on the misogynist who denies a single one, it is to be feared that an aptitude for cards, and least of all Contract Bridge, cannot be numbered. A few stubborn ungracious facts bear out this sweeping statement.

In the whole history of the European championships only three women, Mrs. A. L. (Dimmie) Fleming of Great Britain, Mrs. Vina Spiro of Ireland, and Mrs. Schaltz of Denmark, ever represented their countries. In the history of World championships only one woman, Mrs. Helen Sobel, has ever represented her country, the U.S.A. Since 1932, when Mesdames Watson and Stephenson won the first National Paris Championship of Great Britain, no women's pair has ever won the pair championship of her country outside the U.S.A. In that chivalrous and matriarchal nation it has been won once, in 1947, and let their names be engraved in letters of gold: Helen Sobel and Margaret Wagar. As for the other non-English-speaking countries, it is about as probable that a woman will play on a national team as for a woman to become Emperor of Japan.

On the academic side, only two textbooks in the huge literature of Bridge have been written by women: in England, a treatise on the Nottingham System, which as far as is known, has not materially revolutionized bridge thinking outside the Dukeries, and in America, in the early days, an opus produced by Madeline Kerwin, which one hopes it is not unchivalrous to describe as more curious than valuable.

Despite all this, it is proper to make the *amende honorable* and say equally categorically that the average woman bridge player is a much more skilled performer than the male. It is only in the rarefied atmosphere of expert circles that her inferiority becomes apparent.

The reasons for this are various, the most important being the time at her disposal. The truly devoted female addict will think nothing of playing eight hours a day every day, and to hell with the breadwinner and the children. That does not include the time dedicated to morning coffee when the backs of envelopes and unpaid bills are decorated with hieroglyphics and passed from hand to hand. These represent reconstructions of hands which produced the trials or triumphs of the night before, and form as much a part of the stylized ritual of the Bridge player's way of life as the actual rigor of the game itself.

To enjoy the pleasure of his wife's company the husband, in self-defence, was forced to take up the game, and bridge between the spouses of neighboring families became the social institution which it is to this day.

There can be no doubt that feminine influence, more than

anything else, has been decisive in establishing Contract Bridge as an integral and important part of modern social mores. For example, in latter years, in the United States at any rate, more people habitually sit down for a session of bridge than go to the cinema.

Having noted the influence of women on bridge, the corollary of the effect of bridge on women immediately arises.

Again a paradox presents itself. It may not be true that one of the first laws of female behavior is to make herself attractive to the male, yet it can hardly be denied that no woman deliberately sets out to repel him. This fact makes the three-to-one ratio of women to men bridge players even more astonishing psychologically than mathematically. It defeats the understanding of the ordinary man that his Beatrice, in the sacred cause of beauty, having gone to a salon in the forenoon and subjected her face to an unmentionable mixture of mud and goo, will substitute for that compost a mask of feline rapacity in the atmosphere of a card room.

One dictionary defines a basilisk as a fabulous creature with black-and-yellow skin and fierce death-dealing eyes and breath. This definition provokes the thought that the lexicographer had never frequented a woman's bridge club, or he would have otherwise omitted the word fabulous.

The truth of the matter is that when playing cards women cannot help a facial expression which would freeze the libidinous ardor of the great god Pan himself, for their predatory anxiety makes them bad winners and worse losers.

This is particularly so when the unfortunate husband happens to be the partner, and so well-informed an authority as Albert H. Morehead estimates that seven out of ten bridge games in the U.S. are played between married couples.

World statistics of divorce directly or indirectly attributable to this domestic custom are not, of course, readily available, but it may be of interest to the social researcher to learn that in January 1935 it was announced in the Divorce Court in Budapest that fifty-four marriages were dissolved in Hungary the previous year as a result of bridge playing by women. For a small country this is not unimpressive. It is also of interest to point out that the prewar population of Hungary was seven million; the population of the United States is one hundred and eighty million.

It should not be thought that the men have a clean bill of health in regard to unseemly conduct. The famous Sims-Jacoby face-slapping occurred in a National Tournament, and Culbertson himself was only restrained from attacking Sir Derrick Wernher with his fists during the Lenz match by the timely intervention of Jo.

It is a matter of fact, however, that the only two players charged with committing murder at the bridge table were women. Apart from Mrs. Bennett, Mrs. Henderson of Detroit, Michigan, had the misfortune to play with a partner who pulled the wrong card twice in succession. She expressed her vexation in the only possible way by shooting the lady accurately between the eyes.

This rudeness compares unfavorably with the behavior of Harry Meacham of Wilkesboro, North Carolina. Mr. Meacham had been dealt what seemed like an interminable run of indifferent cards and announced that he would shoot the next man who dealt him a bad hand. It happened to be his deal, and having dealt himself a Yarborough he kept his promise and shot himself through the head.

10

Just Like in a Story Book

The beginning of 1937 marked the zenith of Culbertson's fortunes. The *Gold Book,* aptly named in terms of sales, was published the previous month. His association had made peace with the International Bridge League, and such was his dominance in the bridge world that the overtures had come from the League.

His New Year gift to himself was the Kem Card deal, which together with his other ventures ensured a huge income if he never wrote another word or sold another book. Thanks to his policy over the preceding years of ploughing back every cent of income into the consolidation and expansion of these business enterprises, he had placed them on a foundation solid enough to weather any financial tempest. The same acumen had provided for the future of the children and Jo, although that lady was now very much in the upper income bracket in her own right.

It was at this time that the title Emperor of Bridge was conferred on him, nor was the metaphor far-fetched. Leaving aside a minority of tournament players, almost everyone on the American continent, North and South, played Culbertson, and about ninety percent of teachers taught it. In South Africa, Australasia and the Far East, absolutely no other system was played, and its effect on Europe was expressed by Dr. Paul

Stern, captain of the outstanding Austrian team, in his book *Wir Lizitieren (Thus Bid We)* published that year. "The Culbertson System had shot across like a meteor from the other hemisphere." His books were translated into twelve languages including Arabic and Japanese while his articles were syndicated in every country that could afford a newspaper.

In his autobiography *The Strange Lives of One Man* which ends at the year 1937, Culbertson is more self-revelatory than he thought. He emerges at first on his own evidence as about as egocentric and self-opinionated a character as ever drew breath. This is certainly the impression he left on his contemporaries.

In the early days when his future seemed permanently balanced on the razor's edge and the most desperate fight was for recognition, there was method in his insolence. His consummate psychological flair left him in no doubt that it is better to exasperate authority than be ignored by it.

He would have approved strongly of the impudence of the youthful James Joyce when introduced to Yeats in Dublin's National Library, "I am afraid it is too late for me to influence you," because in a different *genre* this expressed his attitude towards the bridge Establishment and its Official System.

One feels, at the same time, that this was a carefully cultivated facade, an impression strengthened by certain episodes such as his address to the Sales Executive Club, or his frank description in his book of his plan of campaign to capture the public through the media of Sex, Fear and Ego. His methods exhibited a magisterial contempt for mass gullibility, but did not entail a corresponding self-assurance; it will be seen that when the breakup came Jo was the dominant partner.

Whatever contradictions there may have been in his makeup, of two things we may be certain, his utter confidence in his own pre-eminence as a bridge theorist, and his single-minded and consuming ambition which overrode every consideration, and on which his domestic happiness was ultimately to founder.

His stature as a theorist permits no denigration. The best comment upon it is to be found in the fact that every modern system without exception, however artificial or arcane, is founded on the principles he first standardized, because they are inherent in the game and immutable.

From the outset Culbertson was very much alive to the gulf between theory and practice, and to the revealed truth that with the great unthinking public an ounce of the latter outweighed a ton of the former. Hence his really brilliant coup in having the publication date of the *Blue Book* coincide with the Buller match.

During this period he could not afford to relax and the spectacular Lenz match, as well as the Schwab Cup contests, followed. It is as well to remember that the victory over Lenz and the Official System was necessary for survival, in contradistinction from the Schwab Cup matches which were really publicity stunts for himself and his system. The only occasion which he played in a game in which he had a great deal more to lose than to gain was against Sims, and there were two good reasons for it. Firstly, there was the personal animus between the two experts which was real and bitter. In their tournament meetings Culbertson had slightly the better of the argument and never let his antagonist forget it. This ensured its financial success from the start. In the second place, Dorothy Sims was so outclassed as a player by the other three as to make the result a foregone conclusion. For the matter of that, it made the match, as a trial of systems, a complete hoax on the public, the Jo-Ely partnership being so greatly superior as to have been quite capable of winning had they changed systems with their opponents.

These triumphs are the only contests of which the Master writes in his book, leaving the impression on the reader that, excepting the last unfortunate game for the first World Championship, he had never been beaten in an important match, or avoided a serious challenge. This was far from the truth, for while Culbertson had an excellent tournament record, the Four Aces had a better one, so much so that he took care not to accept their challenge although it was couched in the most provocative and insulting terms, worthy of the recipient himself. It even went so far as to offer him a handicap of five thousand points. Culbertson adroitly turned the trick by betting against the sales of their book as against his own, which proved nothing except that "Mike" Gottleib was a better bridge player than a gambler. Yet Culbertson's version, except on the closest reading, is calculated to give the impression that he not only won the bet, which he did, but the match, which he did not, because it never took place.

Another episode about which *Strange Lives* is strangely silent is the match he played against an Austrian team in August 1931. This took place in the course of a tour of Europe with Jo designed to bring the truth to the nations of that Continent, and not least to prepare the ground for his organization. Pursuant to the good work, in Vienna an unofficial match of over 158 hands was arranged with four of that city's leading Plafond players, none of whom had ever before played Contract.

Richard Trierenberg, one of Austria's leading bridge experts, wrote with becoming modesty:

> The main interest of the match was the question as to whether Contract or Plafond should be victorious.
>
> All those taking part were excellent players of great experience, so the actual play of the hands is of only secondary importance, but it must be borne in mind that the Austrian team had to familiarise themselves with Contract and devoted the mornings to this object, and consequently were at the card table twice as long as the American team. Taking this fact into consideration, the Austrian success by 3,850 points is a sound proof of skill.

The Austrian team was Baron von Scudier and Dr. Tafler, and Dr. von Foregger and Dr. von Spanier. One notes that the latter pair represented the Viennese Gentlemen's Club, a fraternity which had few counterparts in the circles in which Ely ordinarily played, and probably gave them an unfair advantage.

The other half of the Culbertson team was Herr Kurt Bendix and Dr. Kurt Berger, two of Germany's leading players, co-opted for the occasion, and although they did not let the side down, they afforded Culbertson the excuse that they were unfamiliar with his methods. Be that as it may, the match gave Culbertson an early and salutary lesson. He never again accepted a challenge: he confined himself to issuing them.

It was during this evangelical expedition that he attempted to indoctrinate the Union of Soviet Socialist Republics.

One cannot but admire the audacity of the American son of a White Russian attempting to start a Contract Bridge industry in a country fast in the triple stranglehold of Joe Stalin, Famine and the New Economic Programme. The result was hilarious.

One would dearly like to read the official Russian version which must, even still, bring a ray of sunshine to the gloomy archives of the Kremlin. We must, however, depend on Ely's.

Apparently, in response to his request, he was courteously given every facility to visit a huge playing card factory outside Moscow with *carte blanche* to ask any questions he wished.

After the conventional vodkas and caviare, the Director of the Russian Card Trust showed him around the great clattering machines attended by hundreds of workers. Ely expressed appropriate appreciation and was brought back to the Director's office where he was shown a graph indicating that sales were down on the previous year by 40 per cent.

He immediately offered to translate the *Blue Book* into Russian and assign the copyright to the Card Trust, an empty gesture as Russia has never signed the Berne Convention anyway.

The offer was politely declined and he was startled to be informed:

"I am afraid you do not understand, Mr. Culbertson. If it goes on like this" (pointing to the graph) "we hope to reduce sales next year by another twenty percent. You must appreciate that our playing card production goal under N.E.P., is zero, and with hard work we can achieve it."

Out of loyalty to the Capitalist system Culbertson forbore to inform the Director that this target had been reached by a great number of Western industries in that bleak year. But he demanded an explanation.

The situation was simple, he was told. From time immemorial the Russians were an inveterate card-playing people and all efforts to stop them had failed. Although under the new dispensation all playing card factories had been closed, and an embargo placed on imports, a vast black market in Swedish cards had grown up. It was then decided that the only course was to create a State Card Trust, with the object of selling as few packs as possible while at the same time freezing out the underground Swedish competition. This could be brought about, it was felt, by making the cards of such inferior quality, design and durability, that the public would eventually cease to buy them. The project had turned the corner and was in sight of success at the time of Culbertson's visit.

It remains to be added that the Soviet is not a member of the World Bridge Federation, nor was Russian one of the languages into which the *Blue Book* was translated.

These were only interludes in a progress of almost continuous success in which Jo was a full participant. By the beginning of 1937, however, the marriage was showing unmistakable signs of wearing thin around the edges. The miracle is that, in spite of a mutual affection, it had lasted so long. Not even Heloise and Abelard had been subjected to greater strain. Devoted as Jo was to Bridge, which was her livelihood even before marriage, she had not bargained for partnering a monomaniac for the rest of her life. Even the *Gold Book* was inscribed:

> To Jo, Bruce, and Joyce
> My future Team-of-Four

This dedication was no doubt felt to be an expression of deepest marital regard, and of the supreme ambition a father could cherish for his offspring. If so, it became clear within a

135

short three months that these fond hopes were unlikely to be realized.

In March 1937 Jo decided to have a chat with her husband. She made her meaning clear. She told him she was fed up with Contract Bridge. When he displayed a shocked incredulity she qualified this by admitting that Bridge was all very well as a game, or even a livelihood, but she had discovered its short-comings as a way of life and a religion. It had probably escaped Ely's notice but aside from being a Bridge partner she was a woman and the mother of two children. Another thing, she was fed up with Ely. Probably the feeling would pass off, she hoped it would, but just now she was fed up with him. Would he please go away. Yes now! Never mind about the World Championship in Budapest, they could meet in Paris and go on there next June.

Although a little bewildered, Ely was as quick on the uptake as the next. He took the hint and the next sailing of the *Normandie* to Europe.

Probably for the first time in his life he was at a loose end. He mooched around the Continent in somber depression. He thought a visit to the South of France to see his brother, Sacha, and recall old times in Russia would cheer him up. He was wrong.

The World Championship was due to start on June 13, and a sick and dejected Ely met his wife at the beginning of the month at Cherbourg. Despite a few days in Paris the reunion was more amicable than amorous, and he described the journey on the Istanbul Express as the most miserable he ever made.

It was not a happy augury for success, but Culbertson's team, which included Helen Sobel and Charles Vogelhofer, played well enough to reach the final, which was more than the other American team, representative of the A.B.L. could do.

In the decider they met the famous Austrian team under the captaincy of Dr. Paul Stern playing his Vienna Club, the first of the really artificial systems whose many misbegotten progeny bedevil and threaten the game today. The Stern methods, based on Culbertson, but with highly stylized refinements, had proved unbeatable over the previous few years, and his team won the first World Championship over the Americans by the not inconsiderable margin of 4,740 points.

At least on this occasion we have two authorities to consult, none other than the respective captains themselves. In his book Culbertson attributes the resounding defeat to a leaden apathy which caused him to play the worst bridge of his life. This does less than justice to his opponents who were almost certainly the outstanding team in the world.

They consisted of the legendary partnership of Karl Schneider and Hans Jellinek, backed up by von Meissl and Fritz Frischauer; and Walter Herbert and von Bludhorn. Each of these names has a place in the history of Bridge and they were fused into a team by the martinet, Paul Stern, until they played like a well-geared machine. In his book *Beating the Culbertsons,* which is written with that judicious impartiality so often displayed by a winner, it is plain that the Americans were beaten by a better team playing a more accurate system.

This was not the view of either Mr. or Mrs. Culbertson, and the former's attribution of defeat to his own shortcomings was received with a more categorical endorsement by the latter than was either politic or wifely.

The highlight came at the international dinner after the Championship. This was presided over by His Imperial Highness the Grand Duke Frederick, and attended by all the contestants together with a bemedalled and bedizened coruscation of Mid-European aristocracy. After dinner it naturally fell to Ely to make the principal speech which, inspired by Imperial Tokay and the flags of the seventeen competing nations, he proceeded to do with some fluency.

Ordinarily Mr. Culbertson was incapable of silence in any one of six languages, but this time the flow of his eloquence was stemmed by a barrage of ill-timed interjections and comments by the usually ladylike Jo. Fortunately, the more punctilious guests did not understand. Ely could hardly believe his

137

ears when they told him it was his helpmate punctuating his most orotund phrases. He treated it as jolly comradely banter but sat down considerably deflated, even less amused than Queen Victoria.

It was the beginning of the end. Although they returned to New York together in September it was to occupy separate floors in the Sherry-Netherland where they lived.

It could not be said that the marriage broke up, it just dissolved, although Culbertson for a month or two deluded himself that this compromise could be put on a permanent basis. In fact, Jo and he did continue as business associates, and even in 1948 in his introduction to the revised *Gold Book* he pays tribute to her as the greatest of all women players, and acknowledges his debt to her as analyst and critic. But the position was hopeless, and in November Jo informed him that she was arranging for a divorce.

It is difficult to withhold sympathy from Culbertson, and it is sad to contemplate a partnership that had survived so many vicissitudes ending in the very year they had achieved almost fairy-tale prosperity. Only eight years previously the *Bridge World* was founded on a hope and a prayer and the snowball began to roll.

Jo's contribution was in many ways as great as her husband's, and to give him his due he always recognized it. If Culbertson built her up as the personification of the ideal woman bridge player, she played the part of Galatea perfectly. Her manners were impeccable, she was easy to look at, cool and chic, and was a really magnificent player. Only Helen Sobel can be mentioned in the same breath as Jo Culbertson.

If Culbertson was responsible for introducing Contract Bridge to every corner of the world, to Jo was due the phenomenon that 75 percent of the players were women. This figure is particularly impressive when it is considered that hardly seventy-five in a thousand played Auction.

While they were complementary to each other as associates, as a husband Ely was quite impossible. At no time had they a home together, and the succession of crises which represented what he regarded as the normal tenor of existence would destroy the equanimity of a Sphinx.

From the day he dictated the last page of the *Blue Book* in a taxi, to the nerve-shattering consummation of the Kem Card deal, through the Buller, Lenz, Beasley and Sims matches, through radio, films, lecture tours, hotels, ships, and tournaments, apart from the daily chores of articles, books and business, life with Ely must have seemed like living on the edge of a volcano in continual eruption.

Jo was anything but a placid woman, she was a highly-strung Irish woman. Something had to snap, and inevitably it was her marriage.

STERN-AUSTRIAN SYSTEM
WORLD CHAMPIONSHIP 1937
BUDAPEST

DEALER NORTH
E.W. VULNERABLE.

NORTH
♠ K J 6 2
♥ A 9 2
♦ J 9 5
♣ K 10 9

WEST
♠ Q 10 9 3
♥ Q
♦ K Q 8 7 6 2
♣ Q 6

EAST
♠ 8 7 5
♥ J 8 7 6 5 3
♦ 10 4 3
♣ J

SOUTH
♠ A 4
♥ K 10 4
♦ A
♣ A 8 7 5 4 3 2

Room 1

North	East	South	West
1 ♣	No	1 N T	No
2 N T	No	3 ♣	No
3 ♠	No	4 ♣	No
5 ♣	No	7 ♣	All Pass

Result: 13 tricks

Room 2

North	East	South	West
No	No	1 ♣	No
1 ♠	No	2 ♣	No
2 N T	No	3 N T	All Pass

Result: 13 tricks

The Vienna System got the Austrians into a bad Grand Slam, which has to make on the lie of the cards.

The Culbertsons' bidding in room 2 is inept.

This hand, the first of the last session of sixteen hands, was the beginning of the downfall of the Culbertsons, who, at that stage, were less than 900 behind. In a frantic search for points they then overbid themselves into further losses.

STERN-AUSTRIAN SYSTEM
WORLD CHAMPIONSHIP 1937
BUDAPEST

SOUTH DEALS.

LOVE ALL.

NORTH
- ♠ K 9 4 3
- ♥ A 9
- ♦ A 10 9 5 4 3 2
- ♣ —

WEST
- ♠ 8
- ♥ K Q 6 2
- ♦ K 8 7
- ♣ Q J 4 3 2

EAST
- ♠ Q 5
- ♥ J 10 7 4
- ♦ Q J
- ♣ K 10 9 7 5

SOUTH
- ♠ A J 10 7 6 2
- ♥ 8 5 3
- ♦ 6
- ♣ A 8 6

Room 1

South	West	North	East
1 ♠	No	2 ♦	No
2 ♠	No	4 ♥	No
4 ♠	No	5 ♦	No
5 N T	No	7 ♠	All Pass

Result: 13 tricks made

Room 2
Bidding identical up to 5 ♦ which was passed out.
Result: 11 tricks made

When Jo passed Ely's asking bid of 5 ♦, on this penultimate hand of the match, it was the last straw. It is also of historical interest, as it was the second last hand they ever played together in their lives; a few months later they were divorced!

11

... *Long Live the King*

Culbertson's dominance over the American and World Bridge scene was so paramount throughout the 1930's that one may be forgiven for overlooking the activities of the other actors. And yet there were some considerable figures, without whose contributions the game could not have developed as it has. They would have been important even in their own right, they became doubly so because of their interaction on the grand Panjandrum.

At the outset there was, of course, the great "Mike" Vanderbilt, and when tournament bridge spread like a forest fire, the famous Four Horsemen appeared. This team consisted of the inimitable giant P. Hal Sims, Willard S. Karn, David Burnstine and, most colorful of all, Oswald Jacoby, the happy warrior of Bridge whose record to this day is unequalled. This combination had an apocalyptic effect on the Duplicate world, their supremacy being such that for four years they were not once beaten in a major tournament. When their incredible run came to an end in December 1931, it caused so great a sensation that the Lenz-Culbertson fracas in the national papers was temporarily overshadowed.

The next constellation in the galaxy were the Four Aces, rather anomalously named as there were more than four of them. They included two ex-Horsemen, Jacoby and David

Burnstine who teamed up with Howard Schenken and Mike Gottleib. Gottleib was later cast into outer darkness by his co-Aces for heretical bidding.

The Aces, thanks to their superb play by the standards of the day, took over where the Horsemen left off, and won all before them. It was galling for them to find that while they were winning everything in sight the golden stream was flowing into Culbertson Enterprises Inc.

In an effort to direct some of the loot into their own coffers, in October 1935 they enlisted the services of "Mike" Jacobs, boxing promoter and manager, to put over a show that would teach Mr. Culbertson (fresh from his Sims bonanza) the facts of life.

Mr. Jacobs deserves a paragraph to himself. It was he who jumped into the ring when Sharkey was adjudged to have fouled Schmeling in his fight for the Heavyweight Championship. Grabbing the microphone he declaimed to the listening millions words which for poignant brevity rank with the Gettysburg Address, "We wuz robbed, we shudda stood in bed."

This impresario brought his talents to bear on the promotion of a bridge match announced as the World's Bridge Championship. The contestants were the Aces, who had now augmented their numbers by the addition of Richard Frey and Mervin Maier, and a French team who had won the championship of the Federation Française du Bridge, enemies of the Culbertson-sponsored Association Française du Bridge-Contract.

He decided that the only arena for such an epic battle was the boxing ring in Madison Square Garden. To obviate any danger of a repetition of accusations of foul play he proposed to place the teams in two soundproof glass cages. To make assurance doubly sure he employed fifty-two pages, dressed as playing cards seven feet high, each of whom would parade around the ring when the corresponding card was played at the table. In this way every one of the fifteen thousand spectators he expected to fill the Garden, would see that the game was on the level.

145

There was only one drawback to these arrangements, no one had thought to inform the French of the imaginative preparations which had been made for their reception. Although he did not understand their remarks, he was hurt and astonished when told that they wanted no part in what they considered an elaborate practical joke in bad taste. As far as they were concerned Mr. Jacobs and his fifty-two animated pasteboards could go jump in the river.

The match took place in a hotel, but "Mike," having booked the Garden, paraded his fifty-two pages anyway. It was not one of his spectacular successes; the uninhabited soundproof glass cages in the ring looked very empty, but no emptier than the auditorium. Mr. Jacobs returned to managing fighters.

The truth of the matter was that Contract Bridge had passed well beyond the crazy stage, as the astute Ely realized. We can only speculate on what he would have done with television, a fascinating thought, but after the Sims affair he knew the golden vein was running out. Bridge was growing up and people preferred to play it themselves, and play it better. From now on the really big money was in teaching them *how* to play it better.

In Philadelphia about this time there was a young and struggling lawyer who saw this fact more clearly than anyone else. He decided to do something about it, and did so to such effect that today his books, writings and methods command a greater public than ever did those of the Emperor himself, whose throne he usurped.

Charles H. Goren was born on March 4, 1901, in Philadelphia, of not very affluent Russian immigrants. By rather more than the usual hard work which was the lot of boys in his circumstances, he obtained an excellent education. He writes a pithy prose which would not discredit Somerset Maugham, his friend and pupil. He gravitated to McGill University in Montreal where he took a first-class degree in law.

It was in McGill that he was invited by a girl friend to join a bridge game. She laughed at his gaucherie and lack of skill.

Goren went home that night and vowed he would never be ridiculed at a bridge table again. He never was.

He devoured every book on bridge he could lay his hands on. He had the very great advantage of having no preconceptions, and he studied the game, unprejudiced, and with the trained analytical mind of a lawyer.

He is the supreme example of the self-made player, and his technique is such as to earn him the title of the experts' expert. There can be no doubt that if Charles Goren were informed that his next partner in the World's Championship was a leading European expert playing an outré artificial system, he would retire to his lair and emerge a week later fully armed for battle.

It is this quality of inhuman concentration that showed him the obstacles that beset the average player. He knew that this person had neither the time nor the ability to take pains to understand the principles which every expert applies. In teaching himself, Goren, as it were, took these principles apart, and saw what made them tick. He then proceeded methodically to systematize them into a code that even the dimmest could understand. In effect, the Goren system does the average player's thinking for him.

Goren would himself be the first to acknowledge his immense debt to Culbertson. There is, in fact, no real difference in kind between the two systems. Even before 1954, when Ely capitulated to the point-count, the only difference was in the method by which players evaluated their hands in making the same sort of bids. In fact, if two teams of experts played a match, one playing Goren and the other Culbertson, it would be found that the bidding in each room would be the same.

The vital and decisive difference lay in simplicity, and the Goren method was by far the simpler and more accurate. Where Culbertson spoke in terms of honor-tricks and plus values, and laid down cumbersome rules for assessing the strength or weakness of the distribution of the low cards, Goren, by translating them into terms of points, reduced the evaluation

147

of both high cards and distribution to a few easy rules which enabled nearly everyone to bid with reasonable accuracy.

For instance, with thirteen Goren points one opened the bidding; with a combined partnership count of twenty-six, game should be bid; enough points to open the bidding when partner has already opened it should ensure game; and so on. Simple in theory perhaps, but its inventor must have been greatly disillusioned by the number of enthusiasts who found difficulty in counting points on their fingers, let alone in their hands.

When Goren returned to Philadelphia from McGill he practiced law. In no other part of the United States, however, not excluding Boston, was the Old Guard so impregnably entrenched in the profession as in the city of brotherly love, and the young counsellor became aware in the course of a year or so that the floor of his office was in no imminent danger of collapsing under the weight of briefs from eager clients. This was the period when Culbertson was proving that there was a fortune in the new game sweeping the country. Goren decided that Contract Law offered a narrower field for his talents than Contract Bridge, a decision for which millions of players have good reason to be grateful.

It would be hard to imagine two personalities more dissimilar than the effervescent Culbertson and the phlegmatic Goren. Two things they had in common, it is true, an astonishing capacity for hard work, and an uncanny talent for appraising the public mind. Even in these regards they differed. Culbertson knew his public with the intuition of the born showman and played on it like a virtuoso on the piano. Goren, on the other hand, through his personal experience knew its difficulties and resolved them, as he had his own, by reasoning and argument.

A great deal of Culbertson's success stemmed from taking the most unimaginable chances, such as founding the *Bridge World* without a penny, or selling the *Blue Book* before he put pen to paper; Goren's genius lay in that aptitude for patience which inspired Buffon's definition: one can no more see him launching himself into a whirlpool like Kem Cards than jumping off the Empire State Building with an umbrella as a parachute.

As the initial step in the long-term campaign for recognition for himself and his methods, Goren whetted his steel on local talent in duplicate tournaments. He sharpened it to such effect as to attract the attention of the great and influential expert, Milton C. Work.

Work is recognized as one of the greatest writers on Bridge. Among his notable contributions to the game was the invention of the Work 4.3.2.1. point-count which Goren was later to adopt and transmute in his own system. He was also one of the most respected figures in Philadelphia society, which was about as accessible to ordinary humans as the Royal Yacht Club. The association was mutually profitable, financially for the doyen, and in experience for the apprentice.

Financially, Work could not have made a better bargain, for with the aid of his industrious and gifted assistant who not merely helped him with his writings and other Bridge activities, but often ghosted for him, in return for a princely $35 per week, his income was boosted to $25,000 per annum. On the other hand, in spite of this parsimony, Goren in the long run was not a loser. The experience he gained as a writer, teacher, and experimenter was to prove invaluable, and it did him no harm to be known as the intimate associate and adviser of the eminent Milton Work.

Soon Goren began to teach on his own behalf, and the freshness of his approach, coupled with his lawyer's clarity of exposition reaped its reward. His adherents became so numerous that he felt equipped to reach for a wider public and in 1936 he published his first book under the almost irresistible title *Winning Bridge Made Easy.* It sold well and the first big hurdle in the race was successfully surmounted. But with what seemed like half the bridge-playing population of the United States festooning the book-stalls with bridge literature, Goren was well aware that a great deal more than authorship of a book was needed before he became a recognized authority.

This "great deal more" was very nearly supplied by Ely himself. For three years Culbertson had been preparing a breathless public for the greatest event in literary history since the printing of Caxton's Bible, the publication of his *Gold Book of Contract Bridge*. From time to time blasts would be blown on the publicity trumpet and the faithful exhorted to be patient for the hour of revelation was at hand; it only awaited the distillation of the last essential drop of wisdom by the master. This sounded a more compelling and less prosaic reason than the real one, which was two-fold *(a)* Mr. Culbertson was employing the exact technique of suspense which was so successful in 1930, and *(b)* he was astutely awaiting the moment when his publishers would inform him that the market was flooded with *Blue Books*. Saturation point was reached eventually, and out came the long promised *Gold Book*.

It was a remarkable achievement and represented the crowning point of Culbertson's career; it is unthinkable that any subsequent treatise on the game could be written without reference to it. The research that went into it was impressive and produced what was really a bridge encyclopedia rather than a textbook. How much of this research was due to his associates and assistants can only be conjectured, but there is no doubt that the stamp of the master is on every page. None but the lyrical Ely could be so inspired with a divine afflatus as to swoon in prose before "the swan-like beauty of the 7.5.1.0 card distribution." And who else among his mundane and pedestrian fellow experts had the cosmic imagination to write of a certain type of hand as "occurring only one in a million Contractual light years?" It speaks well for the literary discernment of the public that it bought over two and a half million *Gold Books*.

Flushed with euphoria Culbertson became rash, and to give the book a send-off which it did not in the least require, he issued a universal challenge to all comers. This was exactly the big break for which Charles H. Goren was waiting and he picked up the gage with almost unseemly alacrity. It was probably this very fact that caused Mr. Culbertson to make enquiries about the brash unknown who showed not merely willingness but impertinent eagerness to meet him in battle. What he discovered he did not like at all. He learned that Milton Work had thought enough of him to let his articles go out under his name, that he was in a fair way of making a big name for himself in the tournament world, but, above all, that he had recently written a damn good book on bridge. This last unpalatable fact was the decider. Ely thereupon did a little calculation which he should have done in the first place.

A less experienced campaigner could appreciate that his antagonist had nothing to lose and everything to gain, and that furthermore he would gain it at Mr. Culbertson's expense. His publishers arrived independently at the same conclusion and delicately enquired if he was deliberately risking sabotaging the sales of the *Gold Book* by taking the chance of losing a totally unnecessary challenge match with the author of a rival system. In Philadelphia Charles Goren received a polite intimation that to Mr. Culbertson's infinite regret he was unable to enjoy the pleasure of meeting him in mortal combat, but a previous and imperative appointment entailed his immediate presence in Europe. Perhaps some other time!

It is ironical to record that seventeen years later, when Culbertson finally and reluctantly geared his system to a point-count which was essentially a *réchauffé* of that evolved by his rival, the latter could find no good reason for accepting an invitation to a challenge match.

Goren's failure to bring Culbertson to battle did not depress him unduly. While recognition had been slow in coming he was forging ahead steadily. In 1937, when his book was beginning to be talked about, he had the good fortune to team up with three fellow citizens who were among the best players in the country. These were Sally Young, John Crawford and Charles Solomon, and together they won the Open Team-of-Four Championship of the United States.

This was still the period when Contract was front page news, and newspaper stories gave prominence to the arrival of a new

151

and forceful personality who was invigorating the game. From now on twenty-four hours in the day were not enough for Goren. He entered for every conceivable tournament, large and small, that was available. He won them all so many times that a recital of his victories would be tedious. In so doing he amassed a sackful of Master Points, currently approaching the seven thousand mark, a total which, for the benefit of the un-initiated, may be compared with the records of Babe Ruth in baseball, or Don Bradman in cricket.

It is amusing, incidentally, that in 1963 his only rival in the master point stakes, and who for a while passed him out, was the erstwhile *enfant terrible* of the early days, Oswald Jacoby.

Again one is struck by the difference in method through which Culbertson and Goren achieved their objectives. The highly-strung, extroverted Ely, while capable of almost terrifying feats of nervous endurance, was never really happy unless enthusiastically engaged in some spectacular tour de force of showmanship. The humdrum grinds of tournament play and writing, although they had to be done, were a drudgery for him. On the other hand, even had Goren the temperament and inclination to adopt the strategy of his antecessor, he could not have done so, for Bridge had passed through the happy crazy days of adolescence. In any event, it is doubtful if Goren ever did anything spectacular in his life, although his success may so be termed; if an athletic metaphor be excused, Ely won the race in a series of dazzling sprints, Goren won his with the persistence of a marathon runner.

Not the least stroke of good fortune which helped him in his journey was the formation of his partnership with Helen Sobel, beyond all argument the greatest woman player today, and the only one capable of competing on equal terms in the very highest class. As has been mentioned, she played in the first World Championship as a young woman; it is a measure of her caliber that the twenty-first anniversary of that event found her partnered by Goren playing against Italy.

Between them they have won every possible prize, and as a

mixed pair are unapproachable. It is a subject of frequent and fruitless argument as to whether she or Jo Culbertson takes first place among women players. Perhaps the fairest comment is that Helen carried on where Jo left off.

Mrs. Sobel's route to the heights of competitive Bridge was to put it mildly, as unlikely as it was circuitous. It is improbable that Contract Bridge was the normal backstage relaxation of the young ladies with whom the then Helen White adorned the Ziegfield Follies. Nor did the Marx Brothers demand a proficiency at the game before engaging her as a *danseuse* in their New York show *The Coconuts*. When she married A. M. (Al) Sobel, another Philadelphian, one of the bright lights of Broadway was dimmed.

Sobel was, and is, a pretty good bridge player, verging on the top rank, but he quickly perceived superior talents in his wife. He therefore abandoned play in tournaments to direct them. He did so with such success that he became tournament manager to the American Bridge League and is described as the greatest director in the game. Helen for her part was to be ranked number one in the U.S. two years in succession. Goren's partner was anything but a dumb blonde.

In the meantime, after the break with Jo, Culbertson had lost his zest for Bridge. His organizations now ran themselves, and the money still poured in from all his enterprises including his books, his newspaper columns, with a vast syndication and largely written by the staff, and such ingenuities as Auto Bridge, a cross between bridge-patience and self-teacher, which netted hundreds of thousands. But for him, all gusto for the hurly-burly of the game had gone for ever.

Searching for an object at which to aim his talents, his restless eye fell upon, of all things, World Peace, a happy choice for a pacifist who was only happy when up to his eyes in conflict.

As far back as 1916, at the age of twenty-five, Ely, who was a member of the American Academy of Social Sciences, gave the world the benefit of his experience in a monograph on sociology which unfortunately has not survived, except perhaps in the

dusty archives of that learned institution. The first fruits of his
labors in an even wider field appeared in the middle of another
war, entitled *World Federation Plan,* and was sponsored by
World Federation Incorporated, of which the author was
Founder President.

This was followed with a tract entitled *World Peace* which,
appearing as it did in the year of Monte Cassino, Stalingrad
and Guadalcanal, might be said to have been somewhat before
its time. The final polemic he discharged in 1946 was *Must We
Fight Russia?*, which was presumably decisive in restraining
President Truman from dropping an atom bomb on Moscow.

Satisfied that the global situation was now cleared up, W. F.
Inc. suspended operations and Culbertson returned to the world
of Bridge to re-assume his mantle of sovereignty.

The following proclamation appeared in the issue of *Bridge
World* for January 1948:

Announcing
THE 1948
CULBERTSON
TEACHERS' CONVENTION
For the first time in eight years teachers and candidate
teachers will have the opportunity to receive personal coach-
ing from
MR. ELY CULBERTSON
Mr. Culbertson's lectures will cover the entire Culbertson
system in the light of latest developments, and important
interpretations and refinements of debated points. Other
leading masters will lecture on special features and expert
technique.

New teachers will be prepared for Culbertson Certificates,
and Certified Teachers will have the opportunity to take their
Masters' examinations.
CULBERTSON NATIONAL STUDIOS

On the back page of the same issue, in announcing his forthcoming book, *Contract Bridge for Everyone,* his first for six

years, he referred to his system "which is used by ninety-eight percent of all bridge players." This was an exaggeration so breathtaking as to be worthy of the imagination of Dr. Joseph Goebbels. The sad truth was that Ely had left his comeback too late and was whistling in the dark.

Had he not been so preoccupied with world affairs he could have seen the writing on the wall four years earlier when Goren replaced him on the *Tribune,* Ely going to the doomed *Sun.* The following year showed Goren's column achieving a larger syndication, but the real body blows did not come until the years 1950 and 1951, with the publication of *Point Count Bidding,* and *Contract Bridge Complete.*

The painstaking and deliberate Goren had delayed publication until he felt his methods could withstand the most rigorous criticism. He even subjected them to close analysis by one of America's leading actuaries. This thoroughness was rewarded beyond his most extravagant dreams, and no adjective short of electrifying would begin to describe the immediate and astonishing impact these books had on bridge players, not merely in America, but all over the world. Some idea of the revolution they effected can be conveyed by the fact that in three years time when Culbertson, surrendering to the current, brought out his version of the point count not one single recognized system anywhere was postulated on any other form of hand evaluation.

The improvement in the standard of the average player was no less remarkable. One accusation can certainly be laid at Goren's door; from the day he published his *Point Count Bidding* a great deal of pure fantasy departed from the game. Among average players meticulously counting their points the days of the two, or even three, thousand penalties were gone for ever. The best they could now hope to do was drop the odd eight hundred, perhaps eleven hundred, points into the opponents' lap, errors of judgment which would have evoked no more than "Bad Luck" from a sympathetic partner when Contract was young and gay.

The most noticeable effect was in the levelling of standards, and it was a levelling upwards. Leaving aside the very best, of whom there are perhaps a hundred in the world, and the very worst, of whom there are a great deal more, bridge players can be roughly graded into categories of expert, good, and average. Each of these categories now implies a much higher degree of skill than in the pre-Goren era, and they tend to approximate to each other as never before.

Formerly, the gulf between the expert and the good player, or the latter and the average, was so great that an uninformed onlooker would be pardoned for assuming that they played different forms of the game. Before Goren to a large extent standardized the bidding, any expert or even good player, could sit down in the company of three club players in the almost mathematical certainty of standing up a winner after the session.

Nowadays, if the run of the cards gives no particular scope for the exercise of expertise, a team of quite modest pretensions can beat a team of world champions over a short match of thirty-two boards. This very thing happened in a tournament to determine who should represent the United States a few years ago, the then reigning champions being unceremoniously dethroned in the very first round by a team of unknowns.

Not all the credit, of course, goes to Goren for this extraordinary advance. Tournament players in insatiable pursuit of their master point status symbols have more and more come in contact with better players, and assimilated their methods, which in turn they transmit to the rubber bridge addicts who form the vast majority. Even in the play of the cards, one finds quite ordinary players executing as a matter of course safety plays, and *coups* that were the prerogative of a few masters such as Lenz or Sims in prewar times. For this technique they can thank the many excellent books on play, and the influence of tournaments.

It would not be true to suggest that the bridge millenium had arrived, and that the day of the system-monger was no more. The fact is that systemania may yet destroy the game.

What is beyond dispute, however, is that thanks to Goren the average player has been given a formula which does most of his thinking for him, and enables him to play the game with a degree of success which was hitherto unthinkable. It is no exaggeration to say, and the records are there to prove it, that four goodish club players playing Goren would have annihilated a team of world experts a quarter of a century ago.

In September 1958 the dominance of Goren was recognized in a full length feature in *Time* magazine, which also caricatured him appropriately on the front cover as The King of Diamonds. This article quoted a few eloquent statistics. In the United States the bridge population had increased by fifteen million to thirty-five million since 1940. As of 1958 Goren's books had sold three and a half million in the U.S. alone and had been translated into eight languages. His column appeared in a hundred and ninety-four newspapers, of which the U.S. accounted for a twenty-six million readership. Finally 90 percent of the full-time teachers in America taught his system.

It also gave an estimate of his income, but one prefers to believe that this is a secret between himself and his God, and, of course, the Internal Revenue Service.

These statistics were never available to Ely Culbertson, who would not in any event have credited them. As late as 1949 he had his head firmly embedded in the sand. Writing in that year's edition of the *Gold Book,* which, despite his remarriage in 1947, preserved its original dedication, he could claim:

"The Culbertson System is today synonymous with Contract Bridge. During the last five years American bridge players have played at least five hundred and twenty-five thousand million bridge hands, if laid end to end they would go round the world fifteen thousand times."

He never lost the cosmic touch.

On December 29, 1955 he died, at the end of the Jubilee Anniversary of the *Blue Book* and the Buller match. Three months later he was followed by a tired and careworn Jo. An unforgettable quarter of a century of Bridge died with them.

157

FINALS EASTERN TEAM OF FOUR
ASBURY PARK, 1932
BRIDGE WORLD V FOUR HORSEMEN

DEALER NORTH

N.S. VULNERABLE

Players, Room 1	*Players Room 2*
N. Von Zedwitz	P. Hal Sims
E. Jacoby	Gottleib
S. Jo Culbertson	Karn
W. Burnstine	Lightner

NORTH
- ♠ —
- ♥ A Q 9 7 3
- ♦ 10 7 5
- ♣ K 6 5 4 3

WEST
- ♠ A 9
- ♥ J 10 8 5 4
- ♦ 9 8 6 4 2
- ♣ 10

EAST
- ♠ K Q J 10 6 5 4 3
- ♥ 6 2
- ♦ —
- ♣ 9 8 7

SOUTH
- ♠ 8 7 2
- ♥ K
- ♦ A K Q J 3
- ♣ A Q J 2

Bidding

Room 1

North	East	South	West
No	4 ♠	All Pass	

Result: Down 1 minus 50

North	East	South	West
No	4 ♠	Double	No
5 ♣	No	No	5 ♠
6 ♣	All Pass		

Result: plus 1390

7 Diamonds is also unbreakable, yet diamonds were never mentioned in either room.

12

Oh! What a Life!

Although out of the millions of players in the world comparatively few take part in competitive bridge, yet their influence on the development of the game has been, and is, inestimable. Speaking generally, they are the most expert. It is their ideas, tempered in the crucible of tournament play, that are disseminated among the great mass of ordinary, average players through books, articles, and personal contact.

Prowess in this form of the game ensures the more ready acceptance of their theories and practice, because of the universal recognition it bestows. For example, the news of the death in New York in August 1963 of Sidney Silidor, a four-time world champion, was broadcast the next morning on the B.B.C.

Further, it does a great deal more than confer the seal of distinction, it is the golden key which opens the door to the big money. The most important single factor in the rise of Charles H. Goren to his position of Bridge supremacy was his amazing record in tournament competition. The vindication of his methods in this ruthlessly cut-throat medium did more to popularize his system then did any other form of publicity.

Two and a half years before *Time* ran its feature on Goren, its associate, *Life,* deputed Marshall Smith to perform a similar service for Tournament Bridge in the United States. The article was entitled *The Savage World of Big Bridge,* a description warranted by the subject. In enumerating the qualities which distinguished the all round big-time players, Smith had recourse to the zoological world, and his compendious inventory catalogues, "The conceit of a peacock, night habits of an owl, rapacity of a crocodile, and sly inscrutability of a snake, memory of an elephant, boldness of a lion, endurance of a bulldog, and killer instinct of a wolf." He required only one member of the fauna family to describe the average player: he is a monkey.

The author goes on to paint an entertaining, if slightly horrifying, picture of the world endenizened by these strange beings for which the laboratory metaphor is as apropos as the jungle, for they put us in mind of a culture of bacilli devouring each other in a bottle.

This highly sophisticated world is the result of a long process of evolution, its book of genesis appearing as far back as 1904. In that year there was published in New York *Analysis and Complete Play of Bridge Tournament Hands* by J. B. Elwell. This is the first book ever written on the subject, and represents a landmark in the story of Bridge, as it was the forerunner of a vast and growing literature. It was the first occasion on which the author engaged the attention of the public—but not the last, for the life (and more partciularly the death) of Joseph Browne Elwell, were in time to intrigue and titillate the entire population of the United States, and arouse such avid speculation as to rank the untimely abridgement of his career among the most fascinating *causes célèbres* in criminal history.

Some sixteen years after the publication of his historic book, to be precise, at 8:35 A.M. on the sunny morning of June 11, 1920, at the urgent invitation of the housekeeper, Mrs. Larsen, two visitors called at a pleasant 14-room brownstone house at 244 West 77th Street, New York City. Although the owner, Mr. Joseph B. Elwell, in dressing gown and pajamas, was sitting in an armchair in his drawing room with an open letter in his hand, he did not rise to greet them. This apparent discourtesy was not resented by the police officers as it was quite involuntary,

Mr. Elwell being immobilized by the presence of a bullet in his head. He was in *articulo mortis,* and died within three hours without becoming conscious.

The police set out to trace his recent movements. In doing so they discovered that he exhibited to a marked degree the nocturnal habits of the owl, which characterize the bridge expert according to Marshall Smith. The previous night had not involved a session at the bridge table. An approximate time-table of his pilgrimage through the night-spots of New York was eventually established.

At about 1:30 A.M. saying he was going home, he parted from his hosts, Mr. and Mrs. Lewisohn, and the latter's sister, Viola, after a supper party at the Ritz-Carlton. The little get-together was in celebration of Viola's divorce from Victor von Schlegel. By a coincidence, or so he said, von Schlegel happened to be sitting at the next table, a circumstance which caused him considerable anguish until Police Headquarters had treble-checked his alibi for the rest of that night and the following morning.

Mr. Elwell did not go home; for him the night was only beginning, and we next hear of him on the New Amsterdam Roof attending the Ziegfield Midnight Frolics, and he later dropped in at the Biltmore for a little good-night dancing. At 4 A.M., he called a halt and the next we know of him was reported by the housekeeper. Three other facts were discovered: his bed had not been slept in, the post by which the opened letter came was delivered at 7:35 A.M. Mrs. Larsen let herself in at 8:15 A.M.

The case bore a superficial resemblance to that of the violent death of another legendary gambler, Arnold Rothstein, some time later. But in Elwell's there was such an embarrassingly rich superfluity of suspects and clues that the police were lost in a wilderness from which they never emerged.

It was clear that robbery was not the motive. The police arrived at this conclusion by the discovery of a few hundred dollars and a set of diamond-studded cuff links on a couch beside the fatal armchair. A doctor at the inquest favored a verdict of suicide, but the corner did not agree as he felt such a finding would involve the theory that the deceased, having shot himself through the head with a forty-five slug from an Army Service Colt automatic, proceeded to dispose of the gun where it was never found, and then sat down in his armchair to read a letter, a sequence of activities which on the whole he regarded as improbable.

The police had independently arrived at the same conclusion and in conjunction with, or rather in opposition to, the District Attorney's office, with which they maintained a running warfare, commenced an investigation that was to cause alarm and despondency among a wide cross-section of husbands, brothers and lovers in New York, and as far South as Lexington, Kentucky. There was also a sharp uprise in the incidence of hysterics among beauteous, if frail, married ladies.

At the time of his death Joseph B. Elwell was probably the leading, and certainly the best known, bridge expert in the United States. But this was not his only claim to public fame. He was as popular in influential circles in Washington as on the racetrack, and he moved in café society as easily as in the exclusive card rooms of the Studio Club, and the venerable New York Whist Club. In general, his way of life was that of a rich man who enjoyed enjoying himself. It also ensured that he knew everyone, and everyone knew him.

He could afford his princely style. When he died he had over $600,000 in liquid assets, to which must be added an income from Bridge, in royalties and teaching, of $25,000, as well as a life interest in a quarter of a million trust fund. Another lucrative harvest was garnered in Wall Street where he had numerous successful flyers. He owned an island at Palm Beach, another place in Long Island, and maintained a racing stable in Latonia, Kentucky. It was a letter from his trainer, Gentry, which he held in his hand when Mrs. Larsen found him.

It was not surprising that he displayed a predilection for the company of pretty women. He was himself suave and good looking, with a head of attractive wavy hair, and he treated them with a charmingly deferential insolence which caused them to flutter their eyes at him, the while their husbands were casting theirs in the direction of the nearest blunt instrument.

This was the Elwell the public knew. The private Elwell was a more complex personality. What the police saw slumped in the armchair was a toothless, bald, rather elderly man. Admittedly, his recent experience was not calculated to improve his looks, but even a revolver bullet would not have caused such a remarkable metamorphosis, reminiscent of Dorian Grey's after his picture was stabbed. The reason, became clear when the detectives found among the deceased's effects an assortment of forty wigs, false teeth, sun-tan lotions, and other aids to masculine beauty.

Nor were these the only surprises laid bare. Leading off Elwell's bedroom was a dressing room furnished like the boudoir of a favored *houri* in the Arabian Nights, and off this room, in turn, was another draped in silk, the most prominent feature of which was a double bed more richly caparisoned than was strictly necessary for inducing sleep. Around the walls was a collection of photographs of over two hundred women.

The D.A.'s office stepped in to join the Homicide Squad. It soon emerged that one of Elwell's more chivalrous practices was to deal out keys to his lady friends like cards at the bridge table. This information was of particular interest to many New York husbands of his acquaintance, who developed an uneasy reflex of stroking their foreheads as if to reassure themselves that they were not the wearers of those cornute adornments which give rise to such regrettable merriment among one's friends.

Nor were the ladies immune from indelicate inquiries. The police, although aware that the musical chairs of Mr. Elwell's love life must have lead to a succession of hell hath no fury scenes, recriminations, and threats, were finally satisfied that the killer was a man. They based this deduction on the not altogether convincing evidence that an army service automatic required an eight pound pull on the trigger; Mrs. Henderson of Detroit was to score a bull on her partner with a similar weapon. William Barnes, Elwell's secretary, produced the convincer by pointing out that his employer would rather shoot himself than appear before any woman without his false teeth and a suitably waved wig.

All the same, both the D.A.'s office and the Homicide squad, before giving up the case as hopeless, had to replenish their stocks of sal volatile for administration to distressed females, overcome by the memories of things past elicited by their inquisitors. Among them may be mentioned a Polish countess, the inevitable Woman in Black, and a belle from Kentucky, whom Elwell had met at the races the previous month. Her father and brother, with true Southern gallantry, had sworn to shoot him even if it meant crossing the Yankee lines north to New York. There was also a famous film actress who spoke tearfully of "That wonderful man Mr. Elwell, he treated me as he treated every woman, like a duchess."

The crime remained on the front page for over a month, and the back page for as long again, but although some very interesting revelations regarding extra-marital diversions among the natives resulted, in the end the authorities surrendered unconditionally.

Their defeat was summed up in an interview with Assistant District Attorney John F. Joyce quoted under the headlines:

INVESTIGATION BLOCKED AT EVERY TURN
ELWELL MURDER BAFFLES POLICE

"There is good reason to believe that one of Elwell's women friends was in the house on the morning of the murder, and that she had good reason to know whether he was killed by an infuriated husband, brother, jealous woman, drunken race track acquaintance, or a bootlegger, and that she does not want to compromise herself."

Incidentally, the only transgressor brought to justice in the case was an unfortunate and indignant small-time bootlegger who was fined $250 for supplying a case of Scotch to the deceased.

The Church, who throughout displayed a very proper interest, pronounced the final judgment on the case. In an address to an enthralled congregation in New York the famous Baptist preacher, Doctor Stratton, dramatically finished his peroration:

This man had turned his home into a harem.

Oh! What a life!

Anyone who has not observed the faithful locked in the fierce embrace of tournament competition will find it hard to understand that marriage, or any other relationship, could founder upon such improbable rocks. Yet history affords us precedents, even if the dedication of the Knights of the Round Table in search of the Holy Grail was not more constant than that of their modern counterparts of the Bridge table in the sedulous pursuit of master points.

Although Elwell recorded the beginnings of the cult, and E. V. Shephard broadcast on Auction as early as November 1923, tournament bridge as it is known today traces to 1927 with the formation of the American Auction Bridge League. When Contract swept the country and proved itself no passing craze "Auction" was omitted, and ten years later, on the signing of articles of peace with Culbertson, it became the American Contract Bridge League, which it has remained ever since.

By reason of the size of America and difficulty of communication in those days, a number of lesser organizations were formed which gradually merged—for example the Pacific Coast association did not do so until 1944, but it was the A.B.L. which gave tournament bridge an impetus.

Under its auspices the master-point system with its ranking of players, later pre-empted by the predatory Ely, was inaugurated. So also were the National Championships for Teams of Four, and Pairs, as well as the Master Pairs Tournament, which are the most coveted prizes in American bridge, and carry the greatest prestige. In addition, there are innumerable congresses and conventions all the year round, some of which attract fantastically large entries. The Master Team Championship held in New York in September 1956 saw 5,600 tables in play.

It is not surprising that early on Culbertson saw potentialities in competitive bridge which had not occurred to his rivals. As ever, his thinking was on the grand scale, and with one of his happiest strokes of genius the first World Bridge Olympic took place in 1932, and was such a success that it was held every year until the war.

The idea was simple, but magnificent. He and Jo prepared sixteen sets of hands, some involving skill in bidding, some in play, and some in both. On each hand par was awarded to the North-South pair and their East-West opponents for obtaining the optimum result, anything else scored nothing. These sets were sent to centers throughout the world where there were sufficient entrants. At 8 P.M., New York time, the seals were broken under the supervision of a director appointed by the national authority of the country, and the hands were bid and played. Valuable prizes were awarded by the Culbertson organization, and the local bodies put up prizes as well.

It is perhaps not an unfair comment on the worldwide standard of bridge at the time to point out that after the scheme had been in operation for six years, and ninety-six hands had been distributed to hundreds of thousands of partnerships, only four pairs in the whole world had obtained par on a set of sixteen hands, and in the previous two years not even one pair.

In this connection it is worth recalling the achievement of Joseph O'Neill of Dublin in the 1936 Olympics. Joe was a fine musician but hardly in the master class as a bridge player. The hands send out by Culbertson had been analyzed and cross-checked by his staff of experts until each and all were satisfied that they were fool proof and susceptible of only one par treatment. On one of them, which involved the declarer placing the singleton King in an opponent's hand, Joe, defending, and having forgotten what were trumps, inadvertently trumped his partner's winning card. This turned out to be the perfect defense to which neither Culbertson nor anyone else had adverted and made it impossible for the declarer to play the hand properly. The result was that red-faced organizers had to send apologies all over the world and cancel the marking for that hand.

The early tournaments of the A.B.L. were dominated by the Four Horsemen team captained by P. Hal Sims, with Karn, Burnstine, and Jacoby. Their *nom-de-guerre* was conferred on them by the columnist, Shepard Barclay, because their feats recalled those of the similarly named footballing combination of Notre Dame which had never played on a losing side. Sims and his henchmen were not beaten until the end of 1931, a remarkable record.

Each of the four was a personality in his own right, and if the gargantuan Sims was the most impressive, Jacoby was the most colorful. His name is part of the history of Contract and forms a link between the days of steam bridge and our age of jet propulsion. This circumstance brings a light relief to the historian's task because it can hardly be disputed that he is the most attractive, the most perverse and mischievous character the game has produced.

His educational background was hardly of a type calculated to develop these qualities. Having read a first-class course in mathematics at Columbia University Jacoby, at the age of twenty-one, became the youngest actuary in the history of that esoteric profession.

He is a firm believer in the axiom that the only certain winner at Contract, or any other card game, is Mr. Percentage, and in 1946 he expounded his doctrine in an opus of humourous and actuarial erudition entitled *How To Figure The Odds*. His mathematical philosophy was succinctly expressed when in referring to the rhetorical inquiry by another bridge expert, the brave Horatius, who asked, "How can a man die better than facing fearful odds?" he commented, "It may be a good way to die, but it's a lousy way to gamble."

If to Dorothy Sims belongs the honor, which no one will wish to dispute, of being the mother of the "psychic" bid, the idea appealed to the anarchistic Mr. Jacoby so much that he became its most inveterate perpetrator. A "psychic" is a bid designed to mislead the opponents into doing something foolish; it often has the same effect on one's partner.

Jacoby's employment of this double-edged weapon has often brought chaos and confusion to the most respectable games. It is also calculated to bring out the beast in the most sedate partners. Jacoby knows by experience for he bears the battle-scars after his bawling-out by his partner in the Lenz-Culbertson match, and the face-slapping by Sims in the Summer Nationals at Asbury Park in 1934.

It must not be thought, however, that because of his non-conformity, Jacoby was not an expert. He ranks as a superlative player, classed number one in the U.S. from 1936 to 1940, and he played in the world championship for the American team in the 1960's.

The Four Horsemen were the predecessors in title of a line of notable successors, and the popularity of the game, and the number of tournaments, steadily increased up to the war. It declined for a few years. Then paradoxically, although less bridge was played, the war did more to spread the game across the world than any other influence since the *Blue Book*.

As any soldier knows, only one percent of war is action, so that in troop ships, base camps, rest camps, P.O.W. camps, and indeed in every part of the globe, Bridge served to relieve the tedium, and not infrequently the terror. The most famous wartime game of all was played in November 1942. The session took place on H.M.S. (blue-pencilled) en route for the invasion beaches of North Africa, and the players were Generals Eisenhower, Gruenther, Clark and Captain Butcher. It is said that the captain engaged in the Tunisian battle with relief—the worst that could happen to him there was to get blown to bits.

One had to wait until about three years after peace broke out for the tournament rat race to run riot. Although an attempt has been made to describe it, nothing short of physical observation can convey the undercurrents of polite ferocity that underlie the smiles of the experts when they aim them at each other. They are out to win.

This ruthless attitude stems from the ingrained conviction of each expert that he is the greatest player in the world. In fact, in the highest echelon there is hardly any difference between the abilities of roughly a hundred of the world's best players. For example, in the first Bridge Olympiad, held at Turin in 1960, after five gruelling final matches involving each country in three hundred nerve-racking hands, France won by one point from Britain. Yet in that series Goren's American team beat France, France beat Britain, and Britain bested the Americans. Results like those do not in any way shake the religious faith of the expert in his own supremacy.

It is further axiomatic that the expert never makes a mistake, at the worst he "takes a wrong view." This infallibility receives admirable expression from Edgar Kaplan, "A mistake in bridge is an action either in bidding or play which in similar circumstances I would not take." John Crawford gave his own version. When asked, "Who in your opinion would be your ideal partner?" he stared at his interlocutor in surprised contempt, "Another John Crawford, of course."

The winning methods adopted by the bridge elite are not necessarily connected with their skill in play or bidding. In an article some years ago entitled *Bridgemanship* Terence Reese, a world-champion and a magnificent player, showed how the ploys advocated by Stephen Potter can be adapted to competitive bridge. Potter, it will be remembered, wrote the delightful *Gamesmanship* or *The Art of Winning Without Actually Cheating*. Reese had obviously learned at the feet of the master.

The article could only have had entertainment value for the master players, because they practised all the tricks already, and a few more besides, such as the baleful Crawford stare, or the active insult of Tobias Stone which earned him a year's suspension by the A.C.B.L., and on another occasion a resound-

ing kick in the bottom from fellow international, George Rapee.
It was also of Stone that the story was told of a partner in an
individual tournament—one in which the rules provide that
each contestant play with every other. When queried as to why
he did not rescue him from an obviously dreadful contract he
replied indignantly, "I haven't spoken to that bastard Stone for
three years, and I'm not going to start now!"

It should be added that Tobias is not by a long way *sui
generis,* and receives honorable mention because he displays
more openly than some of his more restrained colleagues the
killer instinct common to them all.

One might also add that their numbers would be greatly
depleted by the presence of a few Myrtle Bennetts in the major
tournaments. Although contrary to what one would expect, the
best of the women are remarkably well behaved. In spite of the
title of her book, *All The Tricks,* the deportment and manners
of Helen Sobel are impeccable.

One other gift that the pundits share is a frighteningly
accurate card memory. This amounts practically to total recall
and does not lend itself to that Attic salt which seasons the conversation of the finest wits. Indeed, a discussion between two
bridge addicts sounds rather like a dialogue between two electronic computors which someone has forgotten to switch off.
Innumerable anecdotes have been told about this extraordinary
phenomenon, but one that is absolutely authentic is told of
Sidney Lenz and is typical enough to serve for all.

When Lenz, who was incidentally a very kindly man, was
attending the funeral of his friend, Commander Liggett, who
had partnered him in the Battle of the Century, he was heard to
observe sadly, "Poor old Lig, I hadn't seen him for twenty years.
I remember the last time we met. It was at the Whist Club. He
held the Ace, Queen, Knave, and two small spades, the King,
and three small hearts, the King, Queen of diamonds, and two
little clubs."

Even off duty there is no relaxation, and Smith instances two
examples which could be doubled and redoubled. When Lee

Hazen was invited to a yacht for a Caribbean cruise, he complained bitterly that he could never get on deck to enjoy the sun, so a sun-lamp was installed at the next port of call so that the game could continue below. There was also the tournament player who got a wire to say his bereft wife had committed suicide. He booked himself on the later of two planes so that he could continue the game which would "keep me from brooding too much."

Finally, we come to the lesser lights. In the higher flights of Duplicate they merit but a passing reference, as they merely supply the competition, the kudos and the cash for the masterful stars. Reviled with contumely, they are elegantly referred to in competitions as "dogmeat," to be rended to pieces and devoured. This "dogmeat" represents in tournaments the faceless and bewildered millions of ordinary players outside the magic circle.

13

Ah! Wilderness!

While the earliest and primitive form of Bridge was played in England a few years before it crossed the Atlantic, oddly enough it took root in New York at least two years before returning to London. In the words of William Dalton, who was the supreme authority, "Whist was routed root and branch. The triumph of the new game was sudden, complete, and overwhelming."

Slowly at first, but soon in an ever increasing flood, came the spate of books on the game. Here we find that England led the way, although if we except the Bodleian pamphlet *Biritch, or Russian Whist,* the first exposition of the game was printed in New York in 1892. This was snappily entitled *A Short Precis of the Game of Bridge, Drawn Up by Mr. Henry Barbey,* who stipulated it to be for private circulation only.

Mr. Barbey's document, however, can hardly be said to rank as a book, indeed the only existing copy now hangs framed in the card room of the Whist Club of New York. Accordingly, *The Pocket Guide to Bridge* by Boaz, published by Thomas de la Rue in London in 1894, takes precedence as the first textbook on the game ever written. A similar distinction for the Continent attaches to *Traité du Jeu de Bridge* by Henri Pussey, published in Paris in 1901.

From the beginning, the national characteristics of Britain

and America were reflected in their attitude towards Bridge, which became even more pronounced when Auction, in its turn, superseded the older game. The American approach, as one might expect, was based on experimenting with every type of device and convention in the pursuit of accuracy in bidding and in play. In England the game was the diversion of a Society which basked in a halcyon Edwardian sunshine, when the golden sovereign was worth five Yankee dollars, and the only desirable import from the seceded colonies was an adequate supply of marriageable heiresses.

The result was that while the Americans, through a painful process of trial and error, steadily improved their game, in England every transatlantic innovation was met with a fierce and bulldog conservatism. The case for the defence against these newfangled artifices was put in terms of stern intransigence by Dalton in 1908, when he thundered:

"There has lately been a growing tendency among certain Bridge players, chiefly indifferent ones, to put their partners through a sort of catechism before commencing to play.

"Every lover of Bridge, who wishes to maintain the game, as it is at present, the prince of all card games, ought resolutely to set his face against this modern catechism, and to refuse to answer any questions."

In this connection it gives one a glow of pleasure to read that from his strictures this inflexible censor specifically excludes Mr. Elwell of New York, "quite one of the best of the American players."

This dichotomy must always be borne in mind when considering the development of the game; an observation which applies equally to the personalities it produced. It is as inconceivable that a Manning-Foster could have come to the fullness of his bloom in the soil of the United States, as an exotic plant like Culbertson in an English greenhouse.

Tournament bridge, as we have seen, had a paramount influence on the game in America. By studying the results obtained by different players on the same hands, and attempting to eliminate the errors that appeared, a greatly improved technique, particularly in bidding, emerged. Although some reasonably good books were written in England on Auction, nothing approaching the quality of those produced by R. F. Foster, Milton Work, or Sidney Lenz was published there.

This disparity can largely be attributed to the popularity of team matches and pairs tournaments for Auction players in the States, long before Contract was dreamt of. Already in the U.S. Mitchell and Howell had discovered in the early nineties their pairs movements for Whist which are, of course, equally relevant to Bridge. From the beginning, therefore, this form of competition was available to improve the play of even the most ordinary performers. It also had the side effect of producing that multiplicity of conventions aimed at perfection of communication between partners that so aroused the trenchant indignation of William Dalton and his spiritual descendant, Colonel Walter Buller.

In England, tournament bridge was unknown in the clubs, and played only in country houses as a kind of party game. Its status as a serious alternative to rubber-bridge is nicely determined by one of the leading authorities, "Cut" Cavendish, who in *The Complete Bridge Player* devotes three pages to it, as against eleven to a monstrosity called Misery Bridge. This book was published the year after Mr. Elwell had written his text book on Duplicate for American players.

This neglect continued right up to the Culbertson-Buller match, which brought about a transformation. At first, competition was restricted to imitations of this historic contest, partly because teams-of-four matches are simple to play, but mainly because very few had the faintest idea of how to run a pairs tournament.

When, as a result of the interest aroused in competitive bridge by the Buller match, the British Bridge League inaugurated the National Pairs Championship, tournament directors all over the country were initiated into the mysteries of running this type of competition. They spread the knowledge around the local clubs, and the future of competitive bridge was assured.

Its immediate popularity can be gauged from the fact that the membership of the B.B.L. jumped from 280 in its first year to over 3,000 in the second; these figures are the more impressive when it is remembered that while all the members of the League were tournament players, they did not represent one tenth of the number who actually had become converts. By the outbreak of the war Duplicate had ceased to be a novelty in every part of the British Isles.

As we have seen, this state of affairs did not come about without a prolonged exhibition of that maidenly brand of pique and jealousy which Manning-Foster was wont to display whenever he received what he considered an affront to his dignity. Responsible through the Bridge League for the actual establishment of Duplicate on a national basis, he resented the attitude of anyone or any body having the schismatic temerity to organize competitions without first undergoing the ceremony of the laying on of his archiepiscopal hands. In 1934, for example, he refused to act on the committee of the Schwab Cup.

His more usual attitude was one of a magisterial aloofness from the activities of the common herd which made the judicial ignorance affected by his contemporary, Mr. Justice Darling, appear like total involvement. As late as 1937 he informed the Duplicate Bridge Control Board that he had never heard of it, and one searches in vain the prewar files of the *Bridge Magazine,* the official organ of the B.B.L. for any reference to the English Bridge Union, The London and Home Counties Association, or any competition sponsored by the *British Bridge World.*

These last named bodies were all organized by Hubert Phillips and they were more responsible for the spread of tournament bridge throughout the country than was the League.

Phillips has been called, with justification, the father of Duplicate Bridge in Britain, and he certainly did more than anyone else to popularize this form of the game. He made the initial arrangements for the Buller match, and he was so im-

176

pressed by Culbertson's Approach Forcing system that he became an immediate and lifelong advocate of it. As a result, Culbertson found an influential champion and disciple in the editor of the *British Bridge World,* who not only expounded the gospel but spread it effectively by bringing B.B.W. teams to play in every part of England in matches and congresses which he helped to found.

This evangelism, or for that matter, Mr. Foster's, did little to dispel the pure fantastic anarchy which was normal in the general run of tournaments. Had the records of these competitions been preserved for posterity they would fascinate the morbid-minded, and would almost qualify for exhibition in the Chamber of Horrors beside the bloody letters of Jack the Ripper. It was perfectly common for winning pairs on opposite sides in a Mitchell Tournament, which meant that they had been playing the opposing hands, each to be plus thousands of points. If the bidding and play had borne the remotest semblance of sanity such results would be impossible. As it was, they hardly provoked a comment.

As a matter of legal history, the courts were called on to take cognizance of a number of bridge offenses. One important case came before the Liverpool Police Court, where the accused was charged with a serious assault on his partner. Counsel for the defense, while admitting a technical offense, pleaded extenuating circumstances. The Bench, in applying the Probation Act, clearly accepted that the defendant had been subjected to the grossest provocation when it appeared that the complainant had opened the bidding with Two Clubs on the exiguous holding of King, Queen and two small ones. Indeed, one feels that the wrong man was in the dock.

Nor are bridge players themselves averse from invoking the not inexpensive process of the civil courts to arbitrate their disputes. Three times in the last decade they have litigated their grievances in the Royal Courts of Justice in the Strand, on the latter two occasions for libel on their reputation as experts. The most remarkable action of this type, however, was taken against Culbertson in New York when he found himself sued for $100,000 by an indignant plaintiff to whom he had referred as "an average player."

It was fortunate for the expeditious despatch of legal business in the thirties that bridge players as a class did not ordinarily have recourse to the courts to resolve their differences. If they had there would have been such a multiplicity of actions for slander, assault, and other offenses against the person as would have created a backlog of untried cases reminiscent of the chancellorship of Lord Eldon.

The causes for these breaches of the peace are not difficult to discover. Firstly, the standard of card play was, generally speaking, abysmal, and secondly, the standard of bidding was even worse. Brought up on Auction, as most of them were, their minds were conditioned to the methods of that game, with disastrous results. The most noteworthy of these was in the realm of penalty doubles. Playing the older game one could overbid, especially against weaker players, with considerable impunity; under the Contract dispensation such rashness was visited by condign and expensive punishment. A number of astute players soon discovered that they could garner in a great deal more points by allowing their opponents to get out of their depth and then doubling them, than by bidding and making contracts on the strength of their own hands.

It was a lucrative period for the cagey player who knew the value of his cards and was quick on the trigger with his doubles. George F. Hervey, an acknowledged authority on such matters, estimated in 1934 that the big West End players could eke out on average around £3,000 a year from playing bridge—not a bad tax-free income in the hungry thirties. He also recalls in the same article that he saw 500 fr. a point played at Auction in France, about £80 a hundred.

Stakes like these may have enlivened the game in Trouville or Le Touquet; in the hungry thirties even a shilling a hundred was a wild gamble, having regard to the sort of bridge generally played in England at the time. When one realizes the confusion that was rife in American bridge circles, where at least by 1936 the game was standardized on approach-forcing lines, a faint idea of the fog-bound lot of the British may be gathered.

The real fault lay in an almost universal misapprehension of the fundamental principles which even the most esoteric systems must observe. Every newfangled convention was eagerly seized on by the public and while some of them were undoubtedly helpful to the advanced player who knew enough to recognize the conditions proper to their use, the tyro employed them in and out of season to the ruination of his score card and his pocket. Hence the contemporary success of direct methods as advocated by Ewart Kempson, credit for which could be divided equally between his own surpassing card ability and the ineptitude of most of his opponents.

At the same time, and no doubt to prove that he could out-Caesar Caesar, Kempson fathered perhaps the most artificial convention of them all, and one of the most useful: the Kempson Two Club response. It must have tickled his sense of humor to find his brainchild appropriated years later, and reincarnated as the Stayman convention.

From the general confusion at the bridge tables of those days, one must not exempt the actual play of the cards, which earns the sternest animadversions of the historian. One has only to look at the records of the more important matches which have been preserved to shudder that such things could be. Again, when it is remembered that these were the perpetrations of the masters, the mind boggles at the dark deeds that were committed in the name of Bridge in less exalted spheres.

In this branch of the game it is amusing to recall that the average player did not feel that there was the slightest need or room for improvement. In this superstition he was encouraged by the system-mongers who helped to peddle their wares by insisting that proficiency in Contract depended on 90 percent bidding and 10 percent play. Whatever the true ratios were when the standards were so abject, it is now difficult to say. It can, however, be asserted with confidence that nowadays the expert immediately reveals himself less by his bidding than his card technique, although the general ability in both departments has improved out of recognition.

In prewar bridge advanced card technique was very much the prerogative of a small minority, and was only acquired by long experience and study. As for the others, each was convinced that his fairy godmother had visited his cradle for the express purpose of investing him with a lifetime genius for card play. This unearthly endowment was known as "card instinct" and it was a deadly insult to suggest to a player that he was devoid of it. Its assumed possession had also the happy effect of obviating the necessity to read or learn anything about card play other than a few simple rules, mostly derived from Whist. These could be reduced to a very small compass, and mainly consisted of Do's and Don'ts, such as Always Cover an Honor, Third Player High, Second Player Low, Never Finesse Against Partner, and a few other bromides which were as inexorable as the laws of the Medes and the Persians. The deluded addicts totted up their opponents' scores in blissful ignorance that good players depart from these rules as often as they observe them, or that the word "Never" is absent from the expert's lexicon.

There was very little enlightenment to be found in the writings of the pundits. Few newspaper columnists ever devoted an article to the play of the cards, nor between the wars in England was there even one textbook written on the subject.

In America, *Lenz on Bridge* analyzed 257 Auction hands, but this fell far short of meeting the tyro's requirements. In 1934 Culbertson published his *Red Book on Play* which was excellent as far as it went, and his *Gold Book* also contained a helpful section, but not one word on play appears in the *Blue Book*. Louis H. Watson, also in 1934, published the best book on the subject ever written, the classic *Watson on Play,* but its circulation was almost entirely confined to the United States, and in England was read by only those few experts who had least need of it.

Since the war, by a turn of the wheel, many of the best books on play have been British, including another classic, John Brown's *Winning Defence* published in 1952. There may be added *Reese on Play* by Terence Reese, *Card Play Technique* by Mollo & Gardener, and various books by Ewart Kempson, including his Quizzes, each of which is first class, and calculated to improve all but the most instinctive player. All this was in the future. In the meantime a million players stylistically covered each other's honors and led the highest of their partner's suit as if in obedience to a ritual ordained by some higher power.

It is paradoxical that in the midst of this confusion the Acol system, which aimed to synthesize the better elements of direct and approach bidding, was evolving. As we have seen, its humble beginnings in an obscure suburban club gave no promise of the radical effect it was to have on the future of British Bridge.

The facts are eloquent. In the seven years of the European Championships not once did a British team as much as reach the first three. On the postwar resumption Britain won the Championship for the first three years in succession, the European and World Championship in 1954-55, and the European Championship again in 1963. This last event was noteworthy for two reasons. The final British tally, having played each of seventeen countries, was a fantastic 100 victory points out of a possible 102. Of the team of Flint, Harrison-Gray, Konstam, Reese, Schapiro, and J. Tarlo and the nonplaying captain, L. Tarlo, all were prewar Acol players, excepting Flint who was too young to have been. Yet none of these players was a member of the prewar Establishment, nor yet again did their ideas at that time percolate to the lower strata, understandably, perhaps, because in 1938 when the Acol System was first published the British people had other things on their minds.

The activities of the Chancellor of the Thousand Year Reich had had another unforeseen effect on British Bridge the previous year, inasmuch as they were directly responsible for the arrival and eventual domicile in England of a very dynamic character whose influence on the game is still far from being spent. Dr. Paul Stern was in Vienna when the Anschluss was committed in 1937. As a patriotic Austrian, a Jew, and a gentleman, he felt that he had nothing in common with the Führer, so he packed his bags for London. It is pleasant to think that the pain of leaving his beloved Vienna was to some extent mitigated by his pleasure in sending the medals he had won as an officer in the First War to Herr Adolf Hitler in person with a covering note.

It should also be noted that Mrs. Rika (Riksi) Markus, for years conceded to be the best woman player in Britain, was in Vienna at the same time, and reacted similarly.

In both cases Vienna's loss was London's gain, although it is doubtful if this testimonial can be awarded to Paul Stern's contribution to the theory of bidding in Contract Bridge. He expounded this in the Stern-Austrian, sometimes known as the Vienna Club, System which was introduced to the English-speaking public in 1938, the same year as Acol.

It is not generally known that the "Vienna" was not the first system predicated on a cipher code. This term may fairly be applied to a method by which partners communicate information to each other through a series of recondite signals rather than bids related to the suits they actually hold. That dubious distinction historically belongs to the aptly named "Little Joker" system which made a brief and hilarious appearance in 1930 when it disrupted a number of tournaments in the United States.

In this masterpiece of the theorist's art the opening bid of One Club was artificial, as was every one of the partner's responses up to and including Three Spades, denoting the exact number of half-honor-tricks held. The opener then re-bid his hand to show the number of half-tricks he held in excess of three. As the least miscalculation spelt doom, and partnerships were wont to get their wires inextricably and catastrophically crossed, the "Little Joker" never really progressed beyond the teething stage. Modern bidding tendencies being what they are, perhaps its ingenuity will be accorded belated recognition by latter-day bridge-playing cipher clerks.

There were, and are, innumerable systems which embody artificial bids, usually One and Two Clubs, and Slam conventions involving stylized responses. An arguable case can be made out for them, partly, if illogically, because of their universal recognition, but mainly because they are only bricks in the structure of the system rather than forming the very fabric of the structure itself. It was Paul Stern who devised the system to which can be traced those modern meretricious bidding methods which may well be sowing the seeds of the destruction of Contract Bridge in its present form.

Unfortunately the Vienna system in tournament bridge was an unqualified success, if for ordinary players its complexities were much too difficult. We have seen how the Austrian team under Stern's captaincy won the first World Championship, although it is hard to say how greatly this was due to the skill of the players, or the system. In fact, for a part of the final match against Culbertson the Austrians dropped their system, playing ordinary approach-forcing, and still forged ahead. London got its first taste of it the following year when the Austrians easily overcame a strong English team, and the Vienna system had arrived. It is fair to say that to this day it has been employed by experts of the caliber of Messrs Lee and Booker with outstanding success in tournaments of the highest class.

It is ironical that, as Stern himself pointed out, his system stemmed directly from Culbertson. When the latter introduced in the *Gold Book* what he modestly described as the "finest flower of my genius," the Asking Bids, Stern was captivated, and proceeded to build a system around them in a manner that even their imaginative inventor never contemplated.

Until the dawn of the asking bid, partners were instructed to arrive at the best contract by giving each other information regarding their holdings. The innovation was directed not to giving, but obtaining from the partner data as to the specific cards, or distribution of suits, in his hand. As the number of possible bids in Bridge is limited, and strictly limited if the bidding is to be kept safely low, even a nonplayer can see that the lower

183

the level of communication the better, which difficulty Stern dealt with by the employment of bids with a completely artificial meaning. Hence the Vienna System, and the succession of modern and ingenious progeny of which it is the ancestor.

We find at the outbreak of war the Acol system having established a domestic supremacy in English tournaments without making, as yet, any impact on the international scene, together with the genesis of the artificial style of bidding which was to revolutionize international bridge in the fifties and sixties. Neither of these developments had affected to any extent the vast majority of British players, estimated at two and a half million in 1939, who continued to massacre the various systems which they fondly imagined they were playing.

Elsewhere, and that meant all over the world, the approach-forcing system reigned supreme, and through the armed forces, particularly of America, was to penetrate to places of which the much travelled Culbertson had never heard.

During the war itself all was quiet on the tournament front. Thanks to Terence Reese who, with the help of Stern and Selby, formed the Tournament Bridge Association, competitive bridge continued in wartime London. There were also minor tournaments held sporadically in other centers, but by and large activities lapsed. Both the *Bridge Magazine* and the *British Bridge World* suspended publication to reappear postwar in very different guises.

In private houses there was probably more bridge played than ever. A contemporary remark of Reese's is worth recalling, as an example of his rather Whistlerian sense of humor. During a closely fought rubber in a St. James's Club, a terrific crash made the card table jump. One of the players gasped, "My God, they've hit the War Office."

Reese relaxed his concentration for a moment to observe, "Not intentionally, surely!"

If only for this observation wartime bridge had justified itself.

As for the rest, all matches between the countries were, of course, abandoned; for international Bridge the Second World War was the lull before the storm.

14

"We Weep for You . . . "

It is a tribute to the remarkable capacity for punishment of the human race that soon after the outbreak of peace a larger section of it than ever was playing, studying, and even fighting about Contract Bridge. As one would expect, its postwar reconstruction policies were so arranged that playing cards were in general use long before ration cards ceased to be. After all, not by bread alone . . . !

As early as 1946 the Camrose Cup matches, between England, Scotland, Ireland and Wales, were resumed, and September of the same year saw the publication of the *Contract Bridge Journal*. Among the contributors to the first issue were Ewart Kempson, M. Harrison-Gray, S. J. Simon, J. C. Marx, Paul Stern, Boris Schapiro, and an earnest young politician called Iain Macleod.

The editorial introducing the magazine informed the public: "Bridge is no longer a game for the Smart Set, the Professional Gambler, the small fanatical colony of Experts. Bridge has kept minds by the million from dread of air-raids, boredom of prison camps, inertia of troop-ships," and so on.

It goes on to refer to "diehards who maintain that England is capable of selecting an adequate team of English born players without the adventitious aid of ex-mid-Europeans," and rightly comments that, "it would be inconceivable that such

British players as S. J. Simon and R. Lederer should be debarred."

The following month Guy Ramsey, a later editor of the *Journal,* returned to this subject. In dealing with the composition of the "new look" British team, and having suggested that no one should be barred merely because he was an alien, in particular he made a strong plea for the inclusion of Jewish players. One would be inclined to dismiss such advocacy as unwarranted impertinence were it not that a man of the integrity and good feeling of Ramsey would not have indulged in it without good reason. He was obviously reacting against some attempted influence which at the distance of almost twenty years is as obscure as it must have seemed at the time astonishing.

These passages, however, afford the chronicler the opportunity of referring to the debt which Contract Bridge in Britain owes to those very players whose cause it was apparently necessary to plead. The Acol system, which we have seen was the cornerstone of Britain's postwar prestige in the game, was the creation of Marx and Simon. In the last competitions held prewar, three of the Gold Cup winning team were Jews, and Harrison-Gray won the National Pairs partnered by Simon, who played at the Hague on the British team. Since the war, the list is so long as to be tedious, but it is of interest that of the record-breaking British team in Baden-Baden in 1963 no less than three were Jews, including the captain.

On the distaff side, the story is similar except, of course, in the province of pure theory. For years, again including 1963 when it won the Women's European title, the backbone of the British team has been Mesdames "Fritzi" Gordon, and "Riksi" Markus. It is amusing that the latter lady had the pleasure of being three times on the winning side in this championship against Britain when she played for Austria before the war.

Finally, on the question of English-born players it may be pointed out that of the members of the only British team to win the World Championship, Boris Schapiro was born in

Lithuania, and Jordanis Pavlides in Greece; to round off its cosmopolitan appearance it even went so far as to include an Irishman, Adam Meredith.

It is permissible to comment that had chauvinism actuated the postwar selectors rather than good sense and regard for ability, Britain would probably still occupy a similar unfortunate standing in international bridge as distinguished her during the thirties.

On the other hand, in making the statement that "Bridge is no longer a game for . . . the small fanatical colony of Experts," the *Journal* displayed an astonishing naiveté, that is if the tongue were not firmly stuck in the editorial cheek. In point of fact, the direct contrary is true, and the influence of the "small fanatical colony" on the "mind of the million" of ordinary players is such as to threaten the survival of the game, certainly in the form to which it has been developed by the experts.

This situation has come about because of the extraordinary postwar growth of tournament bridge. This has had a radical and equally extraordinary effect on the innumerable players who have never even entered for a bridge contest in their lives. When playing social bridge with tournament players they naturally imitate and adopt the methods which have proved successful in competition, and so, for better or worse, the line of descent from the small fanatical colony is completed. Undeniably, the standard of bidding and play, for this reason, has never been higher, but there is another side to the medal.

The revival and reorganization of tournament and international bridge took place with remarkable speed, in most cases because the patient had not been dead, but merely sleeping. The British Bridge League and the English Bridge Union, all ancient quarrels forgotten, had survived, and their functions were now defined. The Union henceforth controlled all domestic affairs and tournaments (other than the Gold and Portland Cups, reserved to the League) and the other home country organizations were affiliated to it. By 1947 it controlled one

187

hundred clubs and nineteen regional organizations which, by 1963, had grown to thirty-five. The League, in turn, had sole international jurisdiction, representing Britain abroad, and selecting the national teams.

The latter function was for a year or two a sinecure, as the International Bridge League, which had had such a difficult birth, was for obvious reasons a casualty of the war. Fortunately there was in existence no organization analogous to the United Nations to impede the establishment of good relations, and accordingly the European Bridge League was revived, largely through the good offices of the British body, and held its first Championship in 1948.

On the broader international front the Bermuda Cup was first played for in 1950 by teams representing the United States, Europe and Britain. This triangular affair was rather extravagantly described as being for the World Championship, as apparently the inhabitants of Africa, Asia, Australasia, and South America were considered merely as lesser breeds without the law. In 1957 somebody remembered that the Spaniards had discovered South America, and when it was found that there was flourishing in those parts an organization known as the Confederacion Sud Americana de Bridge, it was invited also.

The latest development has been the formation in 1959 of the World Bridge Federation as the supreme international body. The W.B.F. announced that a Bridge Olympiad would be held in every Olympic year starting in 1960, and would be open to every nation. The World Championship for the Bermuda Cup would be held in the intervening years, the Olympic winner competing in the succeeding year only with Europe and the two Americas. This seems a very odd way of determining the championship of the world, but that title in representative Bridge has always been a term of art in any event. Probably the quadrennial tournament is the best form of contest that can presently be devised, and certainly the first Olympiad in Rome, won by France, was highly successful, twenty-nine countries as far-flung as Australia, India, Chile, and Iceland taking part.

All this international activity was really an extension of an extraordinary intensification of public interest in Contract Bridge. In no country was this more striking than in Britain. Indeed, before the end of the war a match between England and the U.S. was broadcast from London and New York, and the B.B.C. was so gratified by the reaction that in 1946 it assigned its ace sports commentator, Stewart MacPherson, to a series of broadcasts featuring Reese, Iain Macleod, and Harrison-Gray. This was a sign of the times for soon Contract Bridge had penetrated to every level of society, and almost every trade and profession had its own clubs, and often its own league, in almost every city in the country, but especially, of course, in London. One of the highlights of Bridge in 1963 was a match between the London Dockers and Crockfords Club, an event which would have gladdened the democratic heart of Manning-Foster.

Due to the travel restrictions of the day, intercourse between the countries was almost nonexistent, with the result that, for at least the first seven postwar years, American, British, and European Bridge developed on distinctive lines. This had incalculable effects upon the development of the game. Broadly speaking, America during this period remained faithful to the approach-forcing methods now transmuted by Goren; England's philosophy was fundamentally Acol; while nobody knew, or cared, what they were up to on the Continent. Both the Americans and the British were due for a considerable shock when they found out!

Two distinctively British books, which were also to affect the native style, came out in 1945 and 1946. These were the "Cab" system invented by Colonel G. G. Walshe, the correspondent of the *Sunday Times,* and the "Baron" system by Leslie Baron and Adam Meredith. For reasons that will always remain obscure to all but a small fanatical colony, these systems created a flutter in the expert dovecote, which to the dispassionate observer appeared a little disproportionate to their content.

British bridge was henceforth to split into two mutually scornful camps in which the Acolites aligned themselves as the protagonists of the well-tried classical principles, and decried the Cab-Baronites as the super-clever products of the age of automation. In fact, the three systems overlapped so much, and each was so resistant to definition, that it was not unusual for partnerships to announce that they were playing Baronized Acol, or Cab, but with Acol no-trumps.

The best comment on this lies in the fact that the arch-priest of Baron, Adam Meredith, even when on the World Championship team, would at the drop of a hat say he was playing either Acol, or Cab without in any way altering the style of bidding. Yet bitter controversies centered around the merits and demerits particularly of Cab and Acol. They even led to a slap-up public challenge match in Selfridges, when Victor Mollo compared the Cab-men, Konstam and Dodds, to footballers playing with their boots on the wrong feet.

The contentions of the big-enders and the little-enders in Gulliver's Travels were not less acrimonious, or less productive of conclusive results. The epic contest proved what was already well known, that all four were first-class players, and that sometimes the luck ran one way and sometimes the other, but the battle continued on other polemic fields.

This discord was strictly a domestic affair, nor was it apparent to profane or foreign eyes. When Britain, under the captaincy of the Acol pioneer, Harrison-Gray, won the European Championship for the first three years of its revival, the team included on each occasion the partnership of Leslie Dodds and Kenneth Konstam who were popularly reputed to say their prayers in Cab before they went to sleep. The prestige of Britain was further enhanced by the victories of the women who in turn won their championships in 1950, '51, and '52.

These were the halcyon days, and although Britain was again to win both championships in 1963, the earlier and unaccustomed fruits of victory were sweeter after the ignominious prewar years of defeat.

It was at this time, however (1948/49) that British bridge lost three of its greatest personalities. Within a period of eighteen months Colonel "Pops" Beasley, Skid Simon, and Paul Stern all died. Looking back to those years we can see that as of that time these three represented the past, the present, and the future.

The past was personified in Colonel Beasley, who as far back as 1905 had written a book *London Bridge* before even the days of Auction. His monument is, of course, the unforgettable match with Culbertson, which would alone reserve a niche for him in the hall of fame. But apart from that glorious hour, he had exercised a considerable influence. With Buller, Kempson, Mathieson *et al.* he was one of the original barnstormers around the country and also devised a system which before the war was widely played.

He was an excellent card player, and as downright as his friendly rival, Buller, with whom he enthusiastically disagreed. Unlike most experts, he was capable of expressing his ideas on other subjects, and did so on at least one historic occasion. It appears that with a typical disregard for good manners, Adolf Hitler caused the announcement of his take-over of the Chancellorship of the German Reich to be made at the precise moment that "Pops" was playing a tricky slam contract in an international tournament being held in Berlin's Adlon Hotel. His concentration ruined, the Colonel immediately stalked to the window and trenchantly addressed a mob of brown-shirts on world affairs in general, and in particular suggesting an appropriate fate for their Führer.

Simon represented the present, and it was a cruel irony that his death took place at the very time that his protegés were translating his theories into a series of unprecedented victories.

It was equally ironical that Paul Stern had also to die at this particular time. For a decade and more he had been chopping and changing his system until even its most faithful devotees were uncertain as to the recommended bid from one day to the next. All this was in the sacred cause of perfect communication and as we have seen, it involved what was then considered the most tortuous artificiality. For this reason his theories never really caught on with the British who, even if they take their pleasures sadly, prefer to divorce them from the strain of mental effort.

It was otherwise on the Continent where, particularly in Italy and France, the agile minds of the experts were concocting systems that would have brought tears of happiness to the eyes of the good doctor who was their mentor and patron saint.

In 1949 there occurred a literary event of the utmost importance to British bridge; the *Bridge Magazine* appeared again for the first time since September 1939, and from there on the contemporary stage may be said to have been finally set.

If anything further had been required to underline the passing of the *ancien régime,* the style and content of the reborn magazine would have surely supplied it. Whereas the magazine of the golden days of its youth reflected the idle thoughts and spacious living of dilettantes who happened to play at Bridge, it now recorded the unremitting activities of a devoted band who played at nothing else.

One wonders what Manning-Foster's reaction would have been had he received articles entitled *The Facts of Strife, The Slam Busters,* or *Cab Is a Many Splendoured Thing.* It is, on the other hand, legitimate to assume that nowadays such effusions as *In Defense of the Fair,* or *Party Bridge* would hardly be accorded the editorial enthusiasm they once commanded, although it is proper to say that a little madrigal by Mrs. Sefi entitled *The Game Is Square,* strikes an authentic modern note, and may yet appeal to the genius of Mr. Elvis Presley.

Gone also, and forever, was the antithetical prose and orotund periods of a more leisured and cultured age. Now men wrote in a strange exotic tongue comprehensible only to initiates of the craft. No longer was the incompetent referred to as a tyro or an average player, he was variously a "palooka," "ham," "mug," or in the United States, "dogmeat." The expression "cold bottom" has no anatomical significance but relates to a poor result in a tournament. Such elegancies as "coffee-housing" for cheating, and "butt in" for overcall, are *comme il faut,* while the adjectives "stiff," "icy," or "dicey," describe the difficulty, or otherwise, of a given contract. The philologist will be surprised to learn that in bridge-playing circles "trance" is now an intransitive verb, meaning to lapse into a state of catalepsy induced by mental indecision at the bridge table.

These and cognate expressions, originally confined to an exclusive caste, are now in common usage in the *lingua franca* of tournament addicts generally. This is as near as they get to admission to the councils of the masters, except vicariously through the glossy columns of the magazines. There are at present two of these, the *Bridge Magazine,* which is the oldest in the world, and the *British Bridge World* which, under the editorship of Terence Reese, took over from the *Journal* in January 1956.

Although the bridge-playing population of Great Britain can be numbered by the million, and those who play in tournaments by the thousand, an uninformed reader of either publication would be pardoned for assuming that Contract Bridge was an exotic activity of a small and strangely devoted band of enthusiasts like Real Tennis or Knurr and Spell. He would also be reminded wistfully of the school mag. he helped to bring out erratically a million years ago. Here also he will find the little private jokes, the sly digs at authority, and every so often an outburst of honest indignation at some real or fancied grievance. Some of this indignation can be quite impassioned and prolonged, particularly between the followers of Acol and Cab, which has lasted pretty well throughout the magazine's reincarnation.

One of the most famous of these controversies was between Harrison-Gray and Dodds, which lasted for months, and inspired a neutralist, Mr. de Guise, courageously to contribute an article entitled *Cabacol (pronounced Cackle)* which supplied much needed light relief, but did not halt hostilities.

A terrifying feature of these wars of words is the ability of either party to produce chapter and verse for actual hands the antagonists played, however long ago. Not even the recording angel is more meticulous, and the expert's dossier is never destroyed. At the same time, however acrimonious they become, it is clear that all are member of the same restricted order, on first name, even nickname, terms. The reader feels almost as embarrassed as though he had opened someone else's letter by mistake. Even their lapses from grace in the interminable round of tournaments to which their way of life inexorably commits them, are reported in those terms of slightly malicious banter which only the closest enemies employ.

Turning to the actual tournaments themselves, it is regrettable to record that they have not always been conducted with due regard for decorum, or happy and friendly rivalry, which should inform such social occasions.

The unforutnate spirit that was becoming all too common was first referred to publicly in January 1951 when the *Journal* reported the British Bridge League as deploring the behavior of certain tournament players. It was, no doubt, a coincidence, and in a different context, that the same periodical the very following month, àpropos the proper attitude to competitive play, expressed the view, "One has to be a killer. The days of kid gloves are over."

In February 1953 a leading commentator said, "In no other game is there such spite, petty bickering, and jealousy." The C.B.J. reluctantly agreed.

In August 1956 when the *Journal* had become the *World,* the editor had the inspiration to publish an article by Godfrey Winn. In a little couplet he gave expression to the benevolent admonishment:

> The World is so full of a number of things
> I'm sure we should all be as happy as kings.

WE WEEP FOR YOU . . ."

One would have thought that the most obdurate heart would have been melted, but incredibly the world was so full of ill-conditioned and badly behaved Bridge players that Terence Reese himself was forced to indite an editorial the following year, which contained the passage:

> Major tournaments, in these days, are like football matches in South America: it is a matter for remark if they pass off without incident and stone-throwing, metaphorical or literal.

Perhaps Mr. Reese was thinking of a not dissimilar incident at a major American tournament when Mr. Tobias Stone appeared to be in imminent danger of decapitation. An infuriated partner, in fact his wife, was in the act of throwing a heavy duplicate board at him, when another terrified competitor shouted, "For God's sake, Stone, don't duck, I'm right behind you."

Tournament Bridge in America was not so affected by the war as it was in Britain and on the Continent. It was to be expected in the immediate postwar decade that it should be of a higher standard, and such was the case. That this superiority was not necessarily permanent should have become apparent in 1949 when a team of top-class Americans played a series of friendly matches against some of the London clubs. It is true that these were played in a social rather than a competitive spirit, but a certain prestige was at stake. While they won four, they should have been warned by the fact that they also lost two to teams employing the modern British style. They were not warned, but on the contrary were satisfied that the well tried American methods, played by experts who had survived the tournament grind, would prove unbeatable.

This complacency appeared to be justified by the results in the World Championship which the U.S.A. won comfortably every year from the date of its renewal in 1950 until 1955.

The result of this dominance was that the intense Bridge activity in Europe escaped American attention. Had this not been the case, later events must surely have seemed less revolutionary.

In Britain and Europe, so far from an atmosphere of complacency, this was a period of experiment, and the testing of new unorthodox ideas. No country could claim to be outstanding, as the results of the European Championships clearly showed. The four championships played in the years 1951-1954 were won respectively by Italy, Sweden, France, and Britain, and the title became more difficult to gain each year.

It was this British team of Dodds, Konstam, Meredith, Pavlides, Reese, and Schapiro that completely outplayed the United States, finally exploded what had become a legend of American dominance, and left them completely bewildered. There was considerable heart-searching, and Alphonse (Sonny) Moyse, the Editor of the *Bridge World,* the most far-seeing and levelheaded of American commentators, expressed the view that perhaps all was not as well as might be with American Bridge.

This mild suggestion may not appear to the uninvolved to be particularly explosive, but the reaction of American bridge players was as if Moyse had suggested that the Union Jack would make a more suitable adornment to the flagstaff on Capitol Hill than the banner of Old Glory. It was generally felt that the setback was only temporary, and that next year would show that American bridge was back where it belonged, at the top.

Next year, in Paris against France, saw the U.S.A. take a comprehensive beating again. This time they got their first taste of the artificial methods which were being worked out in Europe by the ingenious system-mongers. On each occasion, although looking slightly punch-drunk, the Americans took their beating like the good sports they were, although unfamiliarity with the tortuosities of the French canapé bidding system might have afforded extenuation, they did not make excuses. In fact, Charles Goren's sense of humor engaged the affections of the Parisians. When he was asked to buy the complete records of the match for only 100 fr., he inquired:

"What does it cost to destroy them?"

Things were looking serious but worse was to come the following year, 1957, at the Biltmore Hotel, in New York. This time the defenseless Americans were exposed to the full fury of the artificial blitz which was unleashed on them by the European Champions, Italy, and the result was annihilation.

The seemly, if rueful, opening of "Sonny" Moyse's report in the *Bridge World* set the tone for a melancholy tale:

> Well, what is there to say, fellow countrymen, except that we again got licked from hell to breakfast.
>
> The utterly charming and too-darned-efficient Italian team, champions of Europe for 1956, came to New York and trimmed our 1956 United States champions by the not inconsiderable total of 10,300 points.

This was the third successive defeat, and each time by a different European country. Complacency had gone forever. Indeed, some idea of the impact on the country's pride may be formed from the fact that at the third defeat running by Italy, President Eisenhower and General Gruenther were present. The latter had just been appointed Chairman of the World Bridge Federation, and the two great men had an earnest conversation on the subject. This 1959 match was televised and the defeat was witnessed by millions, none of whom took it harder than a colored porter who refused to carry the suitcase of one of the Americans who had played badly.

The next year was the Olympiad, won by France, and then came yet another hat-trick of defeats by Italy in 1961, '62 and '63. Then in 1964 the second World Bridge Olympiad was held in New York resulting in yet another Italian victory. The United States had failed to win a single championship in a decade!

The wheel had turned full circle with a vengeance. Since the days of the original game of Bridge, when nearly sixty years ago William Dalton fulminated against the use of conventions exported from America, that maligned country has been accused of ruining the game with artificiality. This, as we know, was the theme song of Buller and his satellites throughout the thirties, and it was sung by many others also.

In strict truth, however, nearly all these conventions, with some notable exceptions such as the Culbertson Asking Bids, or 4-5 No Trump, together with various Club bids, were merely convenient adjuncts to the bidding of the hand, and in no way fundamental. So far from Culbertson advocating artificial bidding, from the very beginning he devoted his talent for invective to denouncing it on every possible occasion. Thus, the Vanderbilt Club, incidentally an excellent system, and its imitations were at all times targets for his scorn.

His methods triumphed ultimately and became standard practice, particularly in the United States. The Goren methods in these regards differed not at all, and so we find the American game firmly based on a foundation of what is essentially a natural approach in which a spade is called a spade. It can hardly be contradicted that anyone who wished to learn the game today would find it absolutely necessary to be grounded in the Goren methods before branching out on any other system, and the more artificial that system, the more necessary the preliminary groundwork.

In postwar Europe, of course, the case was entirely different. When the Continent was occupied from Spitzbergen to the toe of Italy, and Moscow to the Cherbourg peninsula it can be well imagined that tournament bridge did not rank very high among the popular recreations. When bridge was taken up again the tradition had been broken, and the countries experimenting with new ideas were not impeded by an existing standard practice.

The first fruits of these experiments were displayed at the European Championships in Dublin in 1952, when the Italian Marmic system exploded among the astonished contestants. This was the first important occasion on which a system was built entirely on a codified basis on which the bidding bore no relationship whatever to the players' actual holding. An incred-

ulous player might sit dazed and uncomprehending listening to
his opponents bidding three or four times a suit in which he
himself held all the honors, only to hear him finally name his
real suit after six or seven signals had been exchanged.

Marmic was the opening of the sluice gate. Next year
Canapé, the French contribution to chaos, made its bow, and
then the Swedes came up with an equally obstructive method
mysteriously labelled Efos. Soon the thing became a snowball,
so that when Italy played the U.S.A., in 1957, the three Italian
pairs were playing no less than three different systems, two of
which, christened respectively The Neapolitan Club and The
Roman Club, were of an almost impenetrable obscurity. Just
to make matters difficult, the third pair were playing "Natural"
bridge with the result that Charles Goren was seen to shake
his head in incredulous amazement when an Italian made a
similar bid to one he would have made himself.

In brief, the crossroads of Bridge may be said to have been
reached in the World Championship at Paris in 1956. Since
that date every single championship has been won by a country wedded not merely to a system which embodies artificial
features, but the entire architecture of which is artificial. If
one thing is surer than anything else in an uncertain world, it
is that no "natural" team will ever win a World Championship
against another adopting these methods, that is, of course,
assuming that Bridge will survive at all in its present form,
which is doubtful.

The influence on tournament bridge on the Continent was
immediate, but it bids fair to be no less catastrophic in Britain.
At all times since the war tournament bridge has been played
at every level in an atmosphere of cutthroat intensity. In the
higher levels it means not only prestige but big money. It
means trips abroad for weeks on end to places such as Palermo,
Montreux, Helsinki, Venice, Baden-Baden, Beirut, Paris, with
all expenses paid. One may be taken up by a big playing card
company and flown in luxury to Tokyo, the Philippines, Australia, or where have you. These are but a few of the induce-

ments held out to the contestant to win. There are, in addition, newspaper columns, books, lectures, schools, clubs and so on, and in the United States where the money is really good, television as well. They play to win all right and any legitimate weapon that is available is used.

Even among the lower orders of the hierarchy of bridge, the local tournament players, the rivalry is just as keen. In September 1956 the British copied the American master point system, and the entries for tournaments more than doubled within the year. Today the really fanatical master-pointer, particularly if he lives in a city, will play in a tournament every night of his life in an unremitting greed for pieces of paper which will, probably erroneously, inform the world that he is a better player than his next-door neighbor. In America, where there are roughly two tournaments every day of the year, players have flown three thousand miles to play.

It is this type of player who is the most susceptible to the latest trend, as was pointed out as long ago as 1958 by Victor Mollo. Mollo should know, because he is perhaps the greatest rubber-bridge player, with Edward Mayer, in England. In an article *Bridge Psychology*, Mollo shows the reasons that the Italian methods have a particular appeal for the rank and file, by pointing out that they give them a feeling of being on a level with their betters, and superior to their equals.

The danger to the survival of the game of Bridge has been appreciated for years, as witness just a few of the observations of the Editors of the *Bridge Magazine* and the *Bridge World*.

Ewart Kempson, Editor of the *Bridge Magazine,* is probably the most authoritative writer on Bridge in the world, with a playing and writing experience spanning the whole period of the history of Contract Bridge. He had this to say in his editorial for June 1960:

"I cannot believe that ordinary human beings will want to play a game which requires the constant use of a code book."

In this connection it may be said in parenthesis that one at least of the players on the British team which won the championship in 1963 at Baden-Baden with the aid of an unusually *outré* system, made frequent reference to notes which he carried around in his pocket. This is quite ethical according to the laws.

In August 1960 Kempson again wrote:

"If I went to one of my clubs for a rubber of bridge, and found that one of my opponents was using a highly artificial system of bidding, I would quit. That sort of thing is not a recreation, but merely a boring waste of time. *And I'm quite sure that if it is allowed it will eventually result in the death of the game."*

The attitude of Terence Reese, who was Editor of the *British Bridge World,* was expressed in a letter published in the *American Bridge World* in July, 1960:

"Are your ruling bodies so incapable of seeing the wood for the trees that they lay down requirements in terms of points for a natural call yet allow such nauseating paraphernalia as Stayman responses, transfer bids, Sputnik doubles, and worst of all, psychic controls? It is entirely contrary to the spirit of the game that a player should enjoy the advantages of a bluff bid with almost none of the risks. The one convention we need now is a Geneva Convention to protect players from that and all other forms of poison gas. While just a few bids are left that mean what they say, will you use your influence to eliminate from the game all suit bids that are cyphers bearing no relation to the suit named."

It will be remembered that Mr. Reese could write with all the authority of one of the originators of Acol, apart from being one of the world's really great players.

Finally, George F. Hervey, writing in December 1959, and also a leading authority:

"As the laws are shortly to be revised, one can only hope that the law-givers will see the light; for just as a multiplicity of conventions killed Whist, so the modern multiplicity of conventions is killing Contract.

"It would be a pity to see it crash to death by convention

being piled on convention until the whole top-heavy structure falls with a sickening thud. . . ."

The laws were revised in 1963, for Rubber Bridge as of May 1, and for Duplicate as of July 1. Both sets provide that "Conventional calls or plays should be explained to the opponents before any player has looked at his cards," and in each set there is a saving proviso for the restriction of conventions in games under its jurisdiction. This all means, of course, that the average player in an ordinary rubber is completely unprotected unless the catechism of certain opponents lasts longer than the rubber itself. It is not unfair to say that the rule-making authorities have evaded the real issue.

Mr. Reese, however, has seen the light, or, at any rate, a light. In his column in the *Observer* before the 1936 Championship, he informed his public of the system which he meant to employ, and which he and his associates, Flint and Schapiro had devised. He set out the salient features, which may be of interest to the curio collector.

In this rococo masterpiece One Club denotes a Heart suit: One Diamond equals a Spade suit or a No Trump; One Heart can mean any of these things, exclusive, of course, of a Heart bid; One Spade, strength in Clubs and Diamonds, and One No Trump means, oddly enough, One No Trump. There are other features, and the author informs us that "within this framework the system is complicated. . . ."

This confection is called "The Little Major." Can it be because its ancestor, "The Little Joker," is still protected by copyright?

One may now legitimately inquire: Is there any hope left for the ordinary players?

Probably not.

It is not too fanciful to compare their plight with that of the oysters beguiled from their peaceful beds by those expert conspirators, the Walrus and the Carpenter. The experts indeed have had their pleasant walk, and their pleasant talk, but the tide is slowly stealing up the briny beach.

"O Oysters," said the Carpenter
"You've had a pleasant run!
Shall we be trotting home again?"
But answer came there none——
And this was scarcely odd, because
They'd eaten every one.

London-Dublin

FRENCH CANAPÉ SYSTEM
WORLD CHAMPIONSHIP 1956
PARIS
UNITED STATES V FRANCE

WEST	EAST
♠ A	♠ K Q 7 5 2
♥ 8 6	♥ A Q 7 5
♦ A J 4	♦ K
♣ A K Q J 10 9 3	♣ 8 6 2

WEST (Pierre Ghestem)	EAST (Rene Bacherich)
2 ♣	2 ♦
2 ♠	3 ♦
3 ♥	3 ♠
4 ♣	4 ♠
4 N T	5 ♥
6 ♣	—

It was in the 1956 World Championship in Paris that the U.S., first came up against the artificial blitz.

Although France won, it is pleasant to record that this particular example caused the Americans no pain. It took the French pair 23 minutes to get into the wrong contract, and Lee Hazen asked for a repeat of the bidding, saying:

"I was a young man when it started."

Field and Stayman for the U.S. bid, in one-eighth the time, the Grand Slam thus:

WEST (Field)	EAST (Stayman)
2 ♣	2 ♠
3 ♣	4 N T
5 ♠	5 N T
6 ♦	7 ♣

Actually, there are 13 tricks in N T without a finesse.

THE NEAPOLITAN CLUB SYSTEM
FINALS OF ITALIAN NATIONAL CHAMPIONSHIPS
1956

WEST	EAST
♠ Q X	♠ X
♥ A X	♥ X X
♦ X X X X X	♦ A K X X X
♣ A Q X X	♣ K X X X

WEST	EAST
1 ♦	2 ♣
3 ♣	3 ♦
3 N T	4 ♠
4 N T	6 ♦

This example of the accuracy of the systems of the Italians in the field of slam bidding occurred in their native championships, and is cited by Charles Goren. It can be seen that even if a small spade is substituted for the Queen, the slam can be made —and bid on a combined point count of twenty!

Fortunately for the rest of the world, the part score bidding is not always so precise!

ROMAN CLUB SYSTEM
WORLD CHAMPIONSHIP 1957
NEW YORK
UNITED STATES V ITALY

DEALER EAST
LOVE ALL

                    NORTH
                    Belladonna
                    ♠ 10
                    ♥ K 7 2
                    ♦ A Q J 9 6
                    ♣ A J 8 3

WEST   EAST
♠ J 9 8 7   ♠ Q 6 5 3 2
♥ 10 6   ♥ A 9 8 5 4
♦ K 8 5 4   ♦ 10 3 2
♣ Q 10 2   ♣ —

                    SOUTH
                    Avarelli
                    ♠ A K 4
                    ♥ Q J 3
                    ♦ 7
                    ♣ K 9 7 6 5 4

North	East	South	West
—	No	1 ♥	No
2 ♣	No	3 ♣	No
4 ♦	No	4 ♠	No
4 N T	No	5 ♦	No
6 ♣			

All Pass. *Result:* 6 made

Other Room

3 N T plus 2 by United States.

After their artificial "baptism" in Paris the previous year, the Americans had the doubtful pleasure of encountering the equally recherché Roman and Neapolitan Club Systems on their home ground in 1957.

This example shows the sort of thing they were up against, and in this hand South bids both of East's suits.

At the same time the 3 N T in the other room looks rather gutless.

NEAPOLITAN CLUB SYSTEM
WORLD CHAMPIONSHIP, 1958
COMO, ITALY
ITALY V UNITED STATES

WEST DEALS

E.W. VULNERABLE

NORTH
Becker
- ♠ 9 5 3 2
- ♥ 7 6 5 3
- ♦ 5
- ♣ Q 9 5 2

WEST
Siniscalco
- ♠ A J 8
- ♥ A 10 8
- ♦ A Q 10 9
- ♣ K 10 6

EAST
Forquet
- ♠ Q 10 7 4
- ♥ K J 9
- ♦ J 8
- ♣ A 8 4 3

SOUTH
Crawford
- ♠ K 6
- ♥ Q 4 2
- ♦ K 7 6 4 3 2
- ♣ J 7

West	North	East	South
1 ♣	—	2 ♣	3 ♦
Double	All Pass		

Result: Down 7

Crawford thought he could short-circuit the Italian wiring system. Unfortunately for him, the first two bids had pinpointed every control in the East-West hands. The defense was, accordingly, perfect, and South scored exactly two trump tricks for a loss of 1300 points.

THE LITTLE MAJOR SYSTEM
EUROPEAN CHAMPIONSHIP 1963
BADEN-BADEN
BRITAIN V NORWAY

NORTH DEALS

GAME ALL

NORTH
- ♠ 10 8 7 6 4 3
- ♥ 8
- ♦ Q 7 6
- ♣ K J 9

WEST
- ♠ Q 9 2
- ♥ 7 6
- ♦ K J 10 8 5 3
- ♣ Q 3

EAST
- ♠ A K J
- ♥ A K Q 9 2
- ♦ 9 4 2
- ♣ A 8

SOUTH
- ♠ 5
- ♥ J 10 5 4 3
- ♦ A
- ♣ 10 7 6 5 4 2

North	East	South	West
No	1 ♣	No	1 N T
No	2 ♥	All pass	

The Little Major made his debut with an appropriate fanfare of trumpets in the European Championships 1963. He subsequently appeared at the World Olympiad in New York 1964.

As with all cipher code systems, when things go wrong, they go very wrong indeed. This was not one of the diminutive warrior's more conspicuous successes, as game in the unmentioned Diamond suit is cold.

LITTLE MAJOR SYSTEM
EUROPEAN CHAMPIONSHIP 1963
BADEN-BADEN
BRITAIN V EGYPT

DEALER NORTH

E.W. VULNERABLE

NORTH
- ♠ A 9 5 4 2
- ♥ 9 8 2
- ♦ A K 5
- ♣ K J

WEST
- ♠ J 10 3
- ♥ K 7 5
- ♦ 9 8 6
- ♣ 10 7 4 2

EAST
- ♠ Q 8 6
- ♥ A Q J 10 6 4
- ♦ J 10 4 2
- ♣ None

SOUTH
- ♠ K 7
- ♥ 3
- ♦ Q 7 3
- ♣ A Q 9 8 6 5 3

Room 1

North	East	South	West
1 ♦	2 ♥	3 ♣	No
3 ♥	Double	4 ♣	No
5 ♣	All Pass		

Result: 12 tricks made

Room 2

Egypt bid and made 6 clubs.

The opening bid shows either a spade suit or a strong balanced hand, a feature which is nicely designed to effect subsequent inaccuracy in the auction. It speaks well for the strength of the British team that it could win the championship despite this sort of nonsense.

Index

213